OTHER PEOPLE'S
HABITS

Also by Aubrey C. Daniels:
Bringing Out the Best in People

OTHER PEOPLE'S

HABITS

How to Use Positive Reinforcement to Bring Out the Best in People Around You

Aubrey C. Daniels

McGraw-Hill

New York   San Francisco   Washington, D.C.   Auckland   Bogotá
Caracas   Lisbon   London   Madrid   Mexico City   Milan
Montreal   New Delhi   San Juan   Singapore
Sydney   Tokyo   Toronto

Library of Congress Cataloging-in-Publication Data

Daniels, Aubrey C.
    Other people's habits : how to use positive reinforcement to bring out the best in
    people around you / Aubrey Daniels.
        p.   cm.
    Includes index.
    ISBN 0-07-135915-X (alk. paper); 0-07-137374-8 (pbk.)
    1. Behavior modification. 2. Reinforcement (Psychology) I. Title.
    BF637.B4 D34   2000
    158.2—dc21   00-060925

McGraw-Hill

A Division of The McGraw-Hill Companies

1 2 3 4 5 6 7 8 9 0 AGM / AGM 0 9 8 7 6 5 4 3 2 1 0 (HC)
1 2 3 4 5 6 7 8 9 0 AGM / AGM 0 9 8 7 6 5 4 3 2 1 0 (PBK)

ISBN 0-07-135915-X (HC)
ISBN 0-07-137374-8 (PBK)

This book was set in Garamond by Inkwell Publishing Services.

Printed and bound by Quebecor World/Martinsburg.

McGraw-Hill books are available at special quantity discounts to use as premiums and sales
promotions, or for use in corporate training programs. For more information, please write to
the Director of Special Sales, McGraw-Hill, Two Penn Plaza, New York, NY 10121-2298. Or
contact your local bookstore.

 This book is printed on acid-free paper.

To my family—Becky, Laura-Lee, and Joanna—who played a major role in shaping my habits. I am a far better person because of them.

CONTENTS

CONTENTS

PREFACE

If it is true that knowledge is power, then knowledge of the laws of human behavior must be the most powerful information a person can possess. In the more than 40 years I have worked to improve the effectiveness of organizations, families, and people themselves, I have become convinced that the enormous power of the science and technology of behavior analysis can solve major interpersonal and societal problems.

Because my first two books were oriented toward management, many of our customers asked me when I was going to write a book for all employees. Those requests were the genesis of this book.

In the beginning my working title was *Taking Charge of Your Life*. I started out to write a book to help front-line employees solve interpersonal problems in the workplace. However, as I began writing I realized that it was not a book for front-line employees; it was for everybody. The causes of and solutions to interpersonal problems in the workplace are the same whether you are a clerk or the president of the company, a Sunday school teacher or the parent of a young child or teenager. The causes of and solutions to problems at home and in society are essentially no different from those in the workplace. As a result, this book is written for everybody everywhere.

In this book I have tried to write about the science of human behavior in a way that is interesting, understandable, and as true to the science as possible. To that end I have used many everyday stories about my experiences and those of my professional and business colleagues. I have avoided jargon as much as possible, but sometimes the only way to describe a situation in a manner that communicates clearly is to use the vernacular of the science. I believe you will find that as you get familiar with the few technical terms I have employed, those terms will enrich your understanding of the material and increase your ability to use your knowledge successfully.

To assist you in applying what you learn in this book, I have devoted the Appendix to a number of real-life examples that first appeared in our magazine, *Performance Management*. In those examples, people in all walks of life have successfully solved the widest variety of everyday problems, from family life and sports to government and the community, from the clinic to the classroom.

When you have finished reading this book, you will at the very least understand why people often behave in unusual ways and will have some new ideas about how you can help them and yourself make changes for the better.

Aubrey C. Daniels

ACKNOWLEDGMENTS

I would like to acknowledge the contributions of my family, business associates, and friends because without their stories this book would not have been possible. I would especially like to thank John Domenick, who, as in the past, has provided the encouragement and prodding (antecedents and consequences) necessary to bring a project like this to fruition. He has also edited the case studies in the Appendix and provided valuable hands-on assistance at every stage of this project. Joanne Donner read the manuscript many times, and her suggestions for change always improved the clarity of what I was trying to communicate. Finnur Oddsson and Guy Bruce read the manuscript and made many helpful technical suggestions. Finnur also did research that saved me many hours of work. Many of Gail Snyder's articles from *Performance Management* magazine are included in the Appendix. Not only does she understand the principles and techniques of performance management, she writes in a way that is always clear and interesting.

A
BETTER
WAY

Many people lead bad lives that would gladly lead good ones, but do not know how to make the change.

—Lord Kames, 1760
Quoted in Benajamin Franklin, *Poor Richard's Almanac*

et me begin with a bold statement: Most of the world's problems, from crime and drugs to ineffective education and the threats to world peace, result from a lack of understanding of how consequences change behavior.

While this book is about the science of behavior analysis in everyday life, it deals mostly with the effective use of positive reinforcement. *Positive reinforcement is the most powerful interpersonal tool a person can use to improve a personal relationship, a family, a business, a community, or a nation, yet it is the most misunderstood and misused.* Sad to say, most of what has been written about positive reinforcement is far from scientifically based and probably has done more harm than good.

In various ways and in various places throughout this book I will emphasize the point that the technology on which the book is based—behavior analysis—differs from most popular theories, programs, and systems in that it is a *scientific* approach to managing human behavior. It is a technology for achieving measurable, predictable results. However, to say that behavior analysis is a science and nothing more is like saying that Chateau Lafite is fermented grape juice, a statement which, though technically correct, is scarcely the way one would choose to describe a vintage Bordeaux wine.

Behavior analysis gives us the opportunity to master a powerful and effective technique with which to influence the people around us. Whether at work, at home, or at play, knowing how to deliver positive reinforcement enables us to make changes in our environment that we've been trying to make or wanting to make for years.

This book is devoted to teaching you how to use the power of positive reinforcement to your benefit every day of your life. You will learn how to identify the reinforcers of those around you, why timing is critical to success, and how reinforcement, when properly applied, can change a habit. But before you embark on the truly remarkable journey of discovering precisely how to influence human behavior, there are some things about behavior analysis you should know.

1. First and foremost, behavior analysis recognizes *the true worth of the individual.* Because positive reinforcement must be individualized to be effective, it is impossible for a person to be effective in the long run without treating other people as the individuals they are. This in no way minimizes the important role that groups play in people's lives; instead, it acknowledges that individual performance is what makes groups successful. In fact, *this approach, when properly applied, actually increases the spirit of cooperation* among group members because they do not have to compete with others for reinforcement.

2. The positive reinforcement (R+) approach *does not set limits on what a person can achieve.* Because achievement is behavior, it is available to everyone. The limits caused by genes are small compared to the limits caused by punishment, negative reinforcement, and a lack of positive reinforcement. Even though I have administered many intelligence tests, I have never found them to be a good predictor of achievement. Dr. Anders Ericsson, an authority on acquiring expertise, says,

"The relation of IQ to exceptional performance is rather weak in many domains."[1] Whether with your peers, employees, family, or community, always be ready to reinforce improvement and the results will amaze you much more often than they will disappoint you.

3. The R+ approach *does not judge people on their past but on their current behavior.* I used to have managers in an introductory class in performance management rank their employees from best to worst. Then I told them to keep the lists and predicted that in 6 months someone who had ranked an employee at the bottom of the list would tell me that that person was not only the most improved but was the best performer in the department. In a sizable group of managers, it never failed to happen.

I have seen many instances in which employees on the verge of being fired, employees on whom supervisors had given up, were shaped into outstanding performers. The same types of experiences hold true for teachers and parents. There are hundreds, if not thousands, of examples in which teachers and parents were on the verge of giving up on children behaviorally and academically when, with the use of this technology, they saw rapid and dramatic positive changes in the children's behavior and school performance. Keep in mind that it is very difficult to look at people in their current environment and predict what they will be able to do when they are effectively positively reinforced for improvement.

4. The R+ approach *helps people become self-confident and self-reliant.* Self-confidence results from being positively reinforced for genuine achievement, not from flattery, pep talks, unearned compliments, or positive affirmations. Ben Jonson, the seventeenth-century English poet, wrote, "It is as great a spite to be praised in the wrong place and by a wrong person, as can be done to a noble nature." And almost 350 years later, the prominent behaviorist Dr. B. F. Skinner wrote that

those who help those who can help themselves, work a sinister kind of destruction by making the good things of life no longer properly contingent on behavior. If you have been very successful, the most sententious stupidities will be received as pearls of wisdom and your standards will instantly fall. If you are still struggling to be successful, flattery will more often than not put you on the wrong track by reinforcing useless behavior.[2]

Both Johnson and Skinner were writing about things that destroy a person's confidence and retard his development as a self-reliant, self-reinforcing individual.

5. The R+ approach *reaffirms the morality of the quid pro quo.* Somehow it seems that this nation has come to rely more on the expectation of a free lunch than on the ancient, simple, and manifestly moral quid pro quo: You do this for me; I'll do that for you. We both benefit, neither one at the other's expense. This approach reaffirms the morality of earning what you get by demonstrating beyond doubt that people have higher morale and greater self-respect when they are allowed to earn what they get, whether it's congratulations for a job well done or a substantial cash bonus.

6. The concepts in this book are *universal.* They apply to everybody and every problem. While I do not know how to solve all the problems of living, I know that practically all of them result from inappropriate or ineffective consequences. It doesn't matter where you live or what you do; the behavioral principles apply.

This fact has been proved true time and time again as we have traveled worldwide consulting and leading seminars based on this approach. When we were beginning our work outside the United States, I was somewhat apprehensive about working in a country where we didn't speak the language or know the business customs. As I expressed my concerns to Enrico Ottolini, the person we were training to help with an implementation, he replied calmly, "This will work in Italy." I replied that I was glad to hear it and asked why he was so confident. Smiling, he said, "Because Italians are people, too." Since that time we have implemented this technology in the widest range of businesses in the United States and 18 other countries. We have not had to change the technology one bit because of the nature of the job or where it was done.

So whether in the United States or in a country halfway around the world, whether in a large corporation or in a family of four, the laws of human behavior and the power of positive reinforcement work. By mastering this technology you can be the person who begins a chain reaction of change in your environment. Russell Justice is one of an increasing number of people who are doing just that. Single-handedly, he has brought the power of behavior analysis and positive reinforcement to his family, his community, and his job with the Eastman Chemical Company. He began by applying it at work. He didn't wait until his boss did it to him. He applied it with everybody wherever he was, and he has made and continues to make a significant, positive difference wherever he goes.

Dr. B. F. Skinner summarizes the benefits of such a strategy practiced on a global scale in *Beyond Freedom and Dignity:*

> *It is hard to imagine a world in which people live together without quarreling, maintain themselves by producing the food, shelter and clothing they need, enjoy themselves and contribute to the enjoyment of others in art, music, literature and games, consume only a reasonable part of the resources of the world and add as little as possible to its pollution, bear no more children than can be raised decently, continue to explore the world around them and discover better ways of dealing with it, and come to know themselves accurately and therefore manage themselves effectively. Yet all this is possible.[3]*

This technology is available today. Its power can be realized by anyone who understands the technology and practices it effectively. It calls to mind one of my favorite sayings: "I asked why somebody didn't do something, and then I realized that I am somebody." This is your opportunity to bring the unlimited power of positive reinforcement into your life and into the lives of those around you.

R^+ MEMO	No. 1

The power of positive reinforcement is available to everyone.

Signed _Aubrey Daniels_

2 TURNING BEHAVIOR INSIDE OUT

Nothing so needs reforming as other people's habits.

—MARK TWAIN
Pudd'nhead Wilson

I start one of my seminars by asking the audience, "How many of you have some kind of problem in your life?" They all raise their hands. Then I ask, "How many of you would have fewer problems if somebody else did what he or she was supposed to do?" They all raise their hands again.

It is an almost universal feeling that people don't do what they are supposed to do. People don't work together the way they are supposed to; people don't respect the rights of others the way they are supposed to; children don't behave the way they are supposed to; teachers don't teach the way they are supposed to; employers don't treat employees the way they are supposed to.

Why don't people do what they are supposed to do? Before answering that question, it is helpful to examine some traditional approaches that have been used to explain why people behave the way they do.

WHAT ARE THE TRADITIONAL APPROACHES?

The traditional approaches to dealing with human behavior, and there are many, have all in one way or another appealed to the inner self—the mind—as the source of the problem and the source of the solution. We hear, "That person has to get his head straight," "Her heart is not in it," "He doesn't want it bad enough," "He has low self-esteem," and "She has a poor self-image."

The problem in all these cases is perceived to be "inside" the person. Therefore, the motivation to change must come from within the person. If change must come from within, the question is, "How can people get their heads, hearts, and desires where they need to be?" If a person has a poor self-image or low self-esteem, can that person just will himself or herself to change? Can anybody?

Sigmund Freud, the founder of psychiatry, probably has had more of an impact on the tendency to look inward to find solutions to behavioral problems than anyone else. He taught that behavior stems from "unconscious motivation." Thus, it is hard for a person to know the cause of her or his behavior. The unconscious is so complex and mysterious that only a trained psychiatrist can identify internal conflicts and resolve them through equally complex and mysterious therapy. Those who followed Freud, including the founders of the most popular psychotherapies, such as Adler, Jung, Maslow, and Rogers, have all in one way or another used the same internal-cause theory. Indeed, most current psychotherapies are still based on this approach.

There are at least three problems with internal-cause theories. First, their proposed explanations cannot be verified. Second, they describe situations in a way that doesn't lead to realistic solutions. Third and probably most important, their appeal to changing behavior from within has not worked!

IT'S REALLY AN OUTSIDE JOB

To say that a person is lazy or not motivated does not explain why he or she behaves in a particular way but only provides a general description of that person's behavior. The word *lazy* is a concept that includes a wide range of actions or inaction that range from "not responding quickly to a request" to "not seeking employment." The problem is that although people are comfortable with diagnosing laziness from what they see people do, they have been taught that those actions are caused by something that is wrong with the way a person thinks or feels. Popular psychologists and other writers have publicized the inside-out notion so much that most people accept it uncritically. Consider the following example:

> *Dear Amy,*
>
> *What advice can you give me on how to deal with a friend who never stops talking? Marlene has always been talkative, but every year she seems to get worse. She is at the point of driving me crazy. She talks so much no one in her presence can get a chance to say a word. Even when she asks a question, she will start talking again before the person can answer. Talking to her on the telephone is impossible. You can't get a word in the conversation. If you try, she will talk right over you. She will literally talk for hours.*
>
> *She talks constantly about how her husband never communicates with her and how her friends never seem to have time for her anymore. I know she is lonely, but I'm beginning to feel that I don't have time for her either. I don't want to hurt her, but what can I do?*
>
> *—Too Tired to Listen*

Dear Too Tired,

First you must accept the fact that Marlene is a compulsive talker. She is obviously insecure and anxious and has a deep-seated problem that you can't solve for her. If she doesn't get help with her underlying problems, she will find herself increasingly lonesome because she will eventually drive all her friends away.

The problem with the example of "Marlene, the talker," is that the average person agrees with Amy. After attending one of the seminars we teach at my management-consulting firm practically no one does. In the first place, my students recognize that there is no evidence that this woman is insecure and anxious and no evidence that people who are anxious and insecure talk a lot. In the second place, there is certainly no evidence that there is some problem lurking in her subconscious that is causing her to talk incessantly. Third and most relevant to the problem, most verbal behavior is maintained by a listener. *If there is no listener, most people will not talk.* If people look at someone when they are talking, smile, nod in agreement, and ask questions about what that person is saying, most people will talk a lot. This woman's behavior is not an inside job; it is an outside job. In other words, her behavior most likely is being maintained by sources outside her that are providing reinforcement for her incessant talking.

The good news about changing what someone does is that it is not an inside job. We don't have to delve into somebody's psyche to change annoying, unproductive, or even maladaptive behavior. The most effective way to solve interpersonal problems is to stop looking for internal causes and focus on the problem behavior itself.

This is critical because if the key to changing other people's behavior lies inside them, that makes us somewhat powerless to solve our problems with them. If we say an employee does not produce up to standard "because she is not motivated" or a child does not do his homework "because he is lazy," we are in effect saying that this is just "the type of person they are." It implies that little can be done about it except possibly encouraging the person to take charge of his or her own problem. While it appears that some people are successful at "making up their minds" to change, many others are unable to do so even when the motivation to change is high.

Everybody has known people who have struggled with bad or unproductive habits for a lifetime. Everybody has also been in situations where they have tried everything they knew to solve a difficult interpersonal situation but to no avail. It is no wonder that people give up on trying to change others. They see the only options for dealing with interpersonal difficulties as either to grin and bear it or to get out of the situation. People give up on family relationships, lose friends, quit jobs, or stay in situations in which they are miserable. There must be a better way. A different approach is needed.

BEHAVIOR CHANGE IS THE SOLUTION

Solving all behavioral problems requires that people do some things more often, do some things less often, or do some things differently. In other words, you or someone else, sometimes both, must change behavior in one or more of those ways to solve a problem.

By behavior I mean what a person does. Behavior generally is classified as either verbal (what one says either to others or to oneself) or motor (what ones does, as in a physical act). We are our behavior. Since what people do can be seen by others, behavior is observable. Because behavior is observable, it gives us a more objective assessment of a problem and makes it easier to see whether we are making progress solving an interpersonal problem than it would be if we had to try to get inside someone's brain.

Because thinking and feeling are technically classified as behaviors (private events that can be observed only by the thinker and feeler), they follow the same rules as overt behaviors. However, other people know a person's thoughts and feelings only through observable behaviors.

It is important to distinguish between behavior and the commonly used term *behaving*. When we talk about a child behaving, it usually means that the child is doing what the parents want him or her to do. *Behaving* in this usage is on a continuum of behaving on the one end and misbehaving on the other. However, as used in this book, behavior means anything that a person does, good or bad.

Most of the problems in society, at home, and at work result from behavior—ours or someone else's. What we call work is nothing more than a series of behaviors. Whatever happens at work—good, bad, or indifferent—is the result of behavior. When the sales department tops projections or the programming department solves a software problem, human behavior is the means. When a stack of boxes falls in the storage room, it is also the result of what someone did or did not do.

Major events we are all familiar with are no different. When Neil Armstrong took his historic moonwalk, it was the result of the behaviors of many people over a long period of time. When the Challenger shuttle exploded before our eyes, that too, was the result of human behavior: fatal decisions and subsequent actions surrounding O-ring seals. In short, practically all accomplishments, problems, and circumstances can be traced back to human behavior. In fact, whether an organization succeeds or not is totally dependent on the behavior of its people.

In other words, succeeding or failing at work or in one's personal life is the result of behavior. Whether you have a happy marriage or an unhappy one, a loving family or a chaotic one, it is because of behavior. Whether you feel that you have a satisfying and fulfilling life or one that is devoid of meaning is also the result of behavior. It makes sense, then, that if you understand and can influence human behavior, you can transform your experience in a positive way at work, at home, and at leisure.

CHANGE IS CONSTANT

When your effectiveness or your feelings of well-being are influenced by what others do or fail to do, what can you do to improve the situation? While most people feel powerless to change the behavior or performance of others, they don't realize that in fact they change everybody they come in contact with every day. People are constantly changing. No one stays exactly the same even for a day.

The point is that it is impossible *not* to change people. That fact aside, it is a common perception that one can't change people—not really. As a colleague of mine was fond of saying about various people, "Aw, that fellow was born lazy and has worked hard at it ever since." In other words, that's the way he *is*, and there is nothing you can do to change his basic nature. Well, I'm glad to say my colleague was wrong.

We are all constantly changing the behavior of others. You can't avoid it. If you don't know how you are changing others, you may be changing them in ways that are not helpful to you or them. This book is going to explain how you are changing people now and, more important, how you can use your change power to benefit yourself and those you live, work, and play with. Before I get into the details of how behavior is changed, I want to address some of the thinking that prevents a large segment of the population from taking an active and deliberate role in changing their own behavior and the behavior of those around them.

R⁺ MEMO	No. 2

Don't mess with other people's minds. It's unreliable.

It's not necessary. And it's none of your business,

anyway.

Signed _____

3 BARRIERS TO CHANGING BEHAVIOR

In spite of the fact that everybody has problems with other people's behavior, many people resist attempting to change the behavior of another person. Following are the most common reservations or reasons people have given me over the years for not attempting to change the behavior of others.

PERSONALITY CAN'T BE CHANGED

You've heard comments relating to this thousands of times: "You can't teach an old dog new tricks." "A leopard can't change its spots." "That's just the way he is." These are the things people often say when confronted with behavior that resists attempts to change it.

What is personality? Personality is nothing more than a label for the unique collection of habits that are said to characterize a person. When someone says that a person has a "good personality," she probably is referring to a wide range of behaviors in which that person habitually engages. It may be that the person smiles frequently, gives compliments, offers to help others, tells jokes, or laughs at yours.

When these behaviors happen often, they become habits, and habits consist of a series of behaviors. It follows that if we can change behaviors, we can change habits. If we can change habits, we can change personality. It would be a horrible situation if we were stuck with every bad habit we ever had. We know that old habits can be broken, and if we break enough of them, we will have different personalities.

Someone may counter this by saying, "But I've seen people change their behavior for a short time, only to revert back to their old habits, their old selves." Most people who lose weight gain it back. People quit exercising or start smoking or drinking again. "Doesn't this mean that they really didn't change?" someone might ask. These observations have led people to think that any changes people make in their behavior are mostly superficial and that one's basic personality rarely can be changed in a substantial way.

It is true that when people change their behavior and the new behavior doesn't get enough support to keep it going, the old behavior will come back. New behaviors are fragile and need lots of support—a special kind of support called positive reinforcement that you will learn about later in this book. If people don't get that support, they return to the old, comfortable, or habitual way of behaving.

In spite of the seemingly temporary nature of many behavior changes, everyone knows people who have made substantial changes that have lasted a lifetime. People "got religion," "saw the light," or had a "life-changing event" and made radical changes in their behavior. Some people have stopped drinking after decades of alcohol abuse. Other people have made dramatic changes for the worse: They have gotten meaner! We all know people who have been hurt by divorce, trauma, and illness to the extent that they are soured on humanity, seemingly for a lifetime. The truth is that if we receive enough support for new habits and we maintain them long enough, our personalities will be changed for better or for worse.

PEOPLE HAVE TO WANT TO CHANGE

I hear almost daily, "People have to want to change" and "You can't change somebody unless she first wants to change." If that were true, no one would ever develop negative habits. No one *wills* himself or herself to be miserable in a marriage or on the job. No couple in love goes into marriage wanting to be out of love and facing divorce in a few years. Yet it happens more than anyone would like. The point is that people change all the time even when they don't want to and don't realize they are changing. These changes occur because people are constantly influenced by what people do and say to them. Without our knowing it, the environment influences all of us, all the time.

BEHAVIOR IS NOT AN ADEQUATE GUIDE TO WHAT A PERSON IS REALLY LIKE

Can't people change their behavior but not change their thoughts and feelings? It is certainly possible for people to act one way and feel another. We have all seen people go along with something when we knew their hearts were not in it. The inescapable fact is that we can never know for sure what another person is thinking. The only access we have to their thoughts or feelings is through their behavior: what they say or do. While it's true that someone's behavior is all we have to go by and respond to, it's also true that working with behavior is sufficient for our purposes of changing or influencing a person. In other words, behavior is all we have, but in fact, *behavior is all we need.*

PEOPLE RESIST CHANGE

This is a very common myth about human behavior that is frequently heard at work. The reality is that in most matters people constantly seek change. They want to eat at different restaurants, wear different clothes, go different places, and meet new people. Why, then, do we have the notion that people resist change at work? The answer lies in the fact that most often change at work is associated with disrupting a comfortable way of working. When a new method is introduced, it is more trouble, causes more errors, takes time to learn, and requires more energy and concentration than the old way. Even though the new way may promise an easier time in the future, the immediate impact is most often negative. Huckleberry Finn stated it well when he said, "Well, then says I, what's the use you learning to do right, when it's troublesome to do right and it ain't no trouble to do wrong and the wages is the same."[1]

When the immediate consequences of anything are negative, it is difficult to get a person to do it. When the immediate consequences are positive, people want to change. If someone is having trouble doing something and you show him how to do it differently and the new way works immediately, he will willingly embrace the change and no doubt thank you for your help. However, if the new way doesn't work immediately, he probably will continue to do it the old way.

A good example of the fact that people will not resist change that brings immediate positive reinforcement is a story a pharmaceutical distributor told me regarding the use of two medicines. The first, he said, provided instant relief, but the effect was temporary and masked the disease rather than treating it. The second took several weeks to take effect and had some minor negative side effects, such as nausea. However, it treated the disease. The first medicine outsold the second by a margin of 10 to 1.

CHANGING THE BEHAVIOR OF OTHERS IS CONTROLLING THEM

When people are concerned with control, they are really worried about the connotations the word *control* brings to mind: restriction, repression, domination, and rule. Naturally, normal, healthy individuals would not voluntarily submit themselves to such conditions. In other words, control usually implies conditions where people are coerced to do things they wouldn't do otherwise or are prevented from doing things they want to do.

In another sense, it is impossible to escape controlling the behavior of others. Every time we call someone's name and that person looks up or answers, we have controlled that person's behavior. We got that person to change what he or she was doing and respond to us. If that person didn't respond, he or she controlled our behavior in that we had to call again. However, we don't think of this as immoral or illegal. It is just normal interaction. No one was hurt by it other than by possibly being inconvenienced.

Control is a problem only when some form of force or seduction is used to get a person to do something that is illegal, immoral, unethical, or against a person's best interest in the long run. While it is certainly possible to seduce people to engage in drugs, crime, and other self-defeating and selfish behaviors, I believe that the best defense against that is for a person to learn how to change his or her own behavior and that of others in effective ways. By understanding how to manage behavior, you will learn how to take charge of your life and avoid "being controlled."

The fact is that without some control in a person's life there would be chaos. When control results in a benefit, particularly an immediate benefit, people welcome it. In traffic, for instance, we submit ourselves to considerable control: which side of the road to drive on, when we stop, when we go, and the direction in which we travel. That kind of control doesn't bother us because it works to everyone's benefit by providing smooth and safe travel. By contrast, if people are told they cannot eat in a certain restaurant or join a certain club because of their sex, race, religion, or national origin, that's the kind of control they tend to—and should—reject.

A DELIBERATE ATTEMPT TO CHANGE THE BEHAVIOR OF OTHERS IS MANIPULATION

Can you get people to do things that are not in their long-term interest? Yes, you can. This has been going on throughout recorded history.

Examples of people being seduced into a life of crime and other illegal, immoral, or unethical behavior are as old as history itself. There is no way I would want to teach anyone to be a better manipulator in this sense of the word. However, the more you know about how behavior change takes place, the more you will be able to avoid being a victim of seduction and manipulation. B. F. Skinner said that the best defense against tyranny is the education of all people about the process by which tyranny takes place.

This is not unlike the problem faced by nuclear scientists. Nuclear power can kill; it can also light up a city. Do we deny people the benefit because of the potential danger of misuse? If all knowledge capable of being misused were prohibited, our progress as human beings would certainly be stymied. It follows, then, that if all of us understand the laws of human behavior, we can better ensure that behavior which benefits all of society is promoted and that which is harmful is eliminated.

CHANGE IS UP TO THE OTHER PERSON

If you think that change starts with the other person, you will be continually frustrated in your attempts to bring peace, harmony, and productivity to your family, workplace, and community. To change the behavior of those around you, you must change what you do. By changing what you do, you change the environment for those around you, which in turn changes them.

A good example of this is an experience I had that I like to call "training the trainer." Several years ago I was giving a seminar for Blue Cross and Blue Shield of Alabama. The first half of the day went very well. The time moved quickly, and the audience was very receptive. After the break the pace seemed to slow for some reason, and I noticed that I was favoring the left side of the room. I was conscious that I was doing that and made an effort to address both sides of the room equally, but somehow I always wound up playing to the left side. Finally, one of the attendees raised her hand and let me in on a plan the group had devised during a break.

The class would positively reinforce my walking to the left side of the room by smiling, nodding, and laughing at my jokes. Whenever I would move to the right side of the room, they would start yawning, looking down at their notes, or staring at the clock. We all got a good laugh out of this exercise in behavior change, but the power of its results was clear. My behavior was definitely changed by the behavior of the group, and I didn't even know it.

YOU HAVE NO RIGHT TO CHANGE THE BEHAVIOR OF OTHERS

I have heard people say, "What right do I have to deliberately try to change the behavior of another person?" My answer is, "You are constantly changing the behavior of others anyway. Is it better to change their behavior in ways that you're not aware of that may be counterproductive or harmful?" Examples of people changing the behavior of others for the worse include parents who give in to a child's whining, someone who listens to the chronic complaining of a friend, a spouse who responds angrily to a mate's abusive comments, and an employer who gives a raise to a poor performer.

But even people who are aware of the changes they are trying to make and feel those changes are for the better still ask, "What if I am wrong? What if the change I encourage turns out not to be good for the person?" My response is, "What if you are hurting the person by what you are currently doing or not doing?" Parents continuously face this problem. They ask, "What are the behaviors, values, and dreams that I want my children to have? How do I help my children accomplish them? What if I am wrong?" We can only do what seems best at the moment.

Something that you will learn about behavior is that because it takes many occurrences of a behavior to make a habit, there are many opportunities to correct any errors we make. The fact that most people turn out to be good, moral, and effective citizens is a powerful testamony to the adaptive ability of humans. Making mistakes in our dealings with others is not a problem; continuing to make the same mistake over and over is the problem. No doubt it's been said to you or you have said to others, "I guess you will just have to learn the hard way!" While there are many lessons that we have learned the "hard way," it is not something that we wish on those we love and care for. This book will tell you how to increase the personal effectiveness of all those you know without them having to learn the hard way.

ONLY FEELINGS CAUSE BEHAVIOR

It is radical or at least controversial for most people to read that feelings don't cause behavior. The truth is that feelings are effects of behavior, not causes. This turns out to be an important distinction about feelings and behavior. In fact, probably the best way to change your feelings is to change your behavior.

Most depressed people suffer needlessly because they think that when they start to feel better, they will do more. The reality is when they start to do more, they will start to feel better. If you are depressed and alone at home with your thoughts, getting out and doing something may result in positive reinforcement for other behaviors and that will lift your depression. This is true in the workplace as well. Many people are unhappy at work because they feel unappreciated or unwanted, and they tend to do less work as a result. They think, "When someone notices me, then I'll be able to really produce something worthwhile." The truth is that if they were pro-active about the job and began to show better results, they would find that not only would their feelings about work change for the better, they might begin to attract the appreciation and attention they desire. Behavior first; feelings follow.

In my clinical work it was always more productive to change the problem behavior to behavior that was more likely to be productive (and subsequently more positively reinforcing) than to work through feelings as a precursor to behavior change. If the new behavior results in more reinforcement, positive feelings will follow. If the behavior results in no reinforcement or results in punishment, negative feelings will follow. *Behavior first; feelings follow.*

It is also true that beliefs follow experience. Most people, for instance, will not touch a snake because they imagine it to be cold, slimy, and dangerous. It is only through the behavior of touching a snake and seeing that it is actually dry and warm and usually harmless that one's beliefs about snakes will change. *Behavior first; beliefs follow.*

THE LAWS OF BEHAVIOR DON'T APPLY TO EVERYBODY

Our consulting business started in the south. When we went north, managers said, "I can see how it would work in the south, but we are different up here." That didn't bother me because I had heard that in the south. When we went from one company to another in the south, managers said, "I can understand how it would work in that company, but we are different." That didn't bother me because I had heard that when we went from one plant to another in the same company and to different departments in the same plant or to different offices in the same department. You know what? They are all correct. Everybody is different, *but the laws of behavior respect the fact that everybody is different.* As a matter of fact, it is as a result of the laws of behavior that we are different. Nature will have it no other way.

Whether you are Japanese, German, or French, the laws of behavior work the same. Whether you are white, black, red, or yellow, the laws of behavior work the same. It doesn't matter whether you are a mechanic, the holder of a doctorate, or the chairman of the board; the laws of behavior apply equally to all.

While this list of barriers to changing behavior is not complete, it covers the most common ones. Keep in mind that the items mentioned are not barriers for those who understand behavior and the conditions under which it occurs. It is clear that we can and do change behavior every day. For most people it is an unconscious process, and for many people the manner in which they try to change behavior usually doesn't solve problems. Unfortunately in too many cases attempts to solve problems actually create new ones.

While I don't want to create the impression that we know how to change all behavior, behavior analysis techniques are advanced enough that we certainly know how to change much of the behavior that affects us personally every day. I believe that if you are not completely happy with your world, you have an obligation to change it for the better. This book will tell you how.

(R^+) **MEMO**	No. 3

Since you change people every day, make sure you change them for the better.

Signed

4 THE DEATH OF COMMON SENSE

It ain't so much the things we don't know that get us in trouble. It's the things we know that just ain't so.

—ARTEMUS WARD

There are as many theories of why people do what they do as there are people. Everybody has ideas about what motivates people, why they change, and why they don't. Many of them are wrong. Few are based on solid scientific evidence. As Henry Wheeler Shaw said, "It is better to know nothing than to know what ain't so."[1]

Many of the ideas people have about how to relate to other people come under the heading of common sense. Without formal training we are almost all left to our common sense. The problem is that common sense is not as common as one might think. Common sense is that which everybody assumes, that which seems obvious, that which leaps to the senses. The actions we take in the name of common sense are based on personal experience, not on scientific fact. As such, most of them are dead wrong. Here is a story that illustrates my point.

Many years ago I had a patient who was one of the most self-critical people I have ever seen. She suffered from bouts of depression for many years. Her friends could not understand her depression or constant self-critical statements because she appeared to be living the "American dream."

She grew up in a small town in North Carolina as the daughter of the richest man in town. She was the town beauty queen and the home-coming queen in college, and she graduated magna cum laude. She was married to a doctor and had two beautiful daughters, but even with all this, she didn't seem to enjoy life. She was intensely competitive in all her activities, but winning seemed to give her little pleasure.

In spite of many material gifts from her father, she did not feel that he loved her, and she frequently told stories about him to back up those feelings. One of the most memorable was his reaction when she won the local beauty contest. When she returned home from the contest, which her father had not attended, she approached him in the den where he was watching TV. She exclaimed, "Daddy, I won!" Not joking, he looked at her and said, "I sure would hate to see who came in second." You can imagine how much that comment hurt her.

She used this story to illustrate the point that no matter what she did, she was unable to please him. If she had five A's and a B on her report card, he would respond, "What happened with this B?" When he found out she graduated from college magna cum laude, he asked, "Who was summa?" No matter what the accomplishment, he always made her feel that she could have and should have done better.

While she thought he did not love her, I think he did in his own way. I've seen people like him a hundred times. He reminds me of many of the managers I've observed in my years consulting with corporations. They never have a kind or encouraging word to say to the people around them. Like these corporate managers, this woman's father felt that if you tell people they're doing well, you will make them weak. How many people have you known who believe that if you brag about people, or tell them you are proud of them, they will feel self-satisfied and slack off? A large part of the adult population believes that the way to get the best results and cause people to want to do better is to criticize what they've done and admonish them to try harder next time.

This woman's father had a screwy "commonsense idea" about people. What common sense told him was the right thing to do could not have been more wrong. While his bright, beautiful daughter performed at high levels, we will never know how much more she could have done or how much happier she could have been if her father had understood more about human behavior.

We all come to commonsense conclusions. In fact, common sense misleads everyone every day and in many more ways than in dealing with people.

DOES WALKING MAKE YOU FAT?

A frequent way common sense misleads us is in how we view cause and effect. My friend Wyman has a house on the beach. Every year he takes a group of us to play golf at courses in the area. Golfers get up early to play golf, about the same time as walkers and joggers do. On the third day of a recent golf trip, as we waited at a stop sign for the usual group of walkers to go by, Charlie, another golfer in the group, looked at me and asked, "Does walking make you fat?" Although this was asked in jest (Charlie really does know better), it is a common error people make about cause and effect. Just because two things occur together doesn't necessarily mean that one causes the other. Just because most of the people in the group were overweight does not mean that walking causes people to gain weight.

Another example of common sense leading to faulty conclusions involves the time a few years ago when I was in a rest room that had automatic faucets. When you got close enough to the sink, the water would start to run. By now we all know how these faucets work, but these were among the first such faucets in public rest rooms. As I was washing my hands, I noticed a man approaching the sink. He stopped before he got close enough to the sink to start the water. He was puzzled because he didn't see any handles. There was a soap dispenser on the left side of the sink. Since that was the only thing the man could see to manipulate, he leaned over and pushed the dispenser. When he did, he moved close enough to the sink to activate it. As he was washing his hands, his friend approached and was equally puzzled by what he saw.

On seeing his friend's puzzlement, the first man said, "You have to push the soap dispenser to turn them on." I wondered how many other people they "turned on" to this commonsense conclusion.

How many times have you been turned on to commonsense conclusions? Take the following short "what you think you know ain't so" quiz to find out. (Turn the page for answers.)

1. How long did the Hundred Years War last?
2. What kind of creatures were the Canary Islands named after?
3. In what season of the year did William Shakespeare's *Midsummer Night's Dream* take place?
4. Where do Chinese gooseberries come from?
5. Who discovered Haley's comet?
6. What is the highest temperature in the Arctic?
7. Where does catgut come from?
8. Who invented the automobile?
9. Where did the battle of Bunker Hill take place?
10. Who is buried in Grant's tomb?

As you can see, common sense is not a good guide to much. It is merely the product of unanalyzed experience, much of which is misleading. I give this quiz often in my seminars. At first it seems like a fun exercise, but very often using common sense to make decisions is not fun. The quiz illustrates how people quickly and easily assume something and take it for fact when it has no factual basis. It is disconcerting to me as a behavioral analyst to see how people use similar, unfounded commonsense analyses in daily human interaction, where the stakes are so high. Behavior based on this type of faulty thinking costs businesses billions of dollars every year and contributes to untold misery in human relationships. It is unfortunate that most people think that effective human relationships are the result of nothing but the use of good old common sense.

The noted quality expert W. Edwards Deming continually encouraged managers to make business decisions not from their own experi-

Answers

1. 116 years
2. A breed of large dogs that inhabit the island
3. Early spring: the end of April
4. Also called kiwi fruit; native to New Zealand
5. No one knows; Haley accurately predicted its return
6. Over 90 degrees Fahrenheit
7. Sheep
8. Gottfreid Daimler
9. Breed's Hill
10. Two people: Ulysses and his wife, Julia

ence or from what seemed right at the time but based on data. He accurately observed that experience can teach a person the wrong thing. The fact that you have been doing something for 20 years doesn't mean that you are doing it in the most effective way. The same is true in human affairs. Just because you live a long life doesn't mean that you will have learned to get along with your neighbors or raise a happy family. If that were true, all old people would be wise.

Deming stressed the use of data because he knew how difficult it is for people to separate fact from fiction. As a behaviorist, I certainly know how true that is when it comes to human behavior. Psychology has not been very helpful here. Although one can find wisdom in the ages and I quote much of it, separating wisdom from folly can be done only through a special kind of experience. That kind of experience is generally called science. Its value lies in the fact that it is systematic and data-based. When we approach human behavior in this way, we can see if what happens is due to what we did or observed or to other, less obvious factors.

If you do not understand behavior as a science, you will be constantly frustrated with people at work, in the community, and at home. This does not mean that you have to be a researcher in behavior analysis, but it does mean that if you are to be successful with others you need to know some of the basic laws and principles of behavior. As we have already discussed, one can't rely on common sense to make decisions. There must be a better way.

Systematic data-based experience can teach you a great deal. When I was a clinical psychology intern, I was interrupted one Saturday morning by a message that Mrs. A., one of my patients, was in the emergency room at the hospital and I should come immediately. When I arrived at the hospital, I saw Mrs. A., whom I had interviewed earlier that week, sitting in the treatment room with her wrists bandaged. She had cut them with a razor blade in an apparent suicide attempt. When she saw me, she started sobbing.

Her life was a shambles. She was involved in a messy love affair with a neighbor. Unhappy in her marriage and unable to leave it, she was depressed most of the time. On this day suicide seemed the only way out. Since I was an inexperienced therapist, I tried everything I could think of that might be helpful. For over 2 hours I listened, analyzed, reflected, and interpreted.

After I had exhausted my repertoire, I called my supervisor and discussed disposition with him. To my astonishment he recommended that I send her home! I protested, but he insisted, and I had no choice. I must admit that when she left, I had no idea what she would do. I didn't know whether she would kill herself, her husband, or her lover. My anxiety was sky-high. I even looked in the Sunday paper to see if she had finished the job.

Her regular appointment was Tuesday morning. She was late, and that of course heightened my anxiety. Suddenly she burst into my office and exclaimed, "Oh, Dr. Daniels, you'll never know how much you have helped me." As I looked at her I thought, "Lady, you are absolutely right. I have no idea what I did, if anything, that helped you, and I couldn't do it again if my life—or yours—depended on it."

To this day I don't know if anything I did on that Saturday really had a significant impact on her behavior. There could have been many other things that had more of an impact than my session. It could have been something that a neighbor, her husband, her lover, or her minister had done. Although she thought I had done something important, it is quite possible that it was insignificant in producing her behavioral change.

Certainly there was little that I learned from this experience. Since I had done everything I knew, the only possible learning I could get was to do everything I knew with every patient I ever saw from that day on. That would not be efficient or satisfactory to my patients or me. What I later learned was that I should have had her try one thing, track it, evaluate its success under several conditions or situations, and then try something else. In this way I could find out what worked and what didn't. I was lucky in this particular situation, but had I known what I did right, I would have been able to apply my learning to future patients.

If we don't take a systematic approach to solving problems with people, we will never be able to generate consistent results with those with whom we work and live. It is imperative to develop a basic framework that will help us better understand not only why people do what they do but also how to change what they do in ways that are beneficial to them and to us.

A SCIENTIFIC APPROACH

The material in this book is based on research that has been conducted over the last 80 years. In my work over the last 30 years I have applied these research findings in the widest range of situations, including mental health, juvenile delinquency, education, family and marital counseling, and, for the last 25 years, all aspects of business.

Some people fear a scientific approach to anything because scientific laws seem to imply a lack of freedom and a lack of emotion or feeling. However, by understanding the laws of behavior and acting in concert with them, you will be able to protect and enhance your own life and the lives of those close to you.

The following passage is from a book by the Nobel Prize-winning physicist Richard Feynman:

I have a friend who's an artist, and he sometimes takes a view which I don't agree with. He'll hold up a flower and say, "Look how beautiful a flower is. But you, as a scientist, take it all apart and it becomes dull." I think he's kind of nutty.

First of all, the beauty that he sees is available to other people—and to me, too. I believe, although I might not be quite as refined aesthetically as he, I can appreciate the beauty of a flower. But at the same time, I see much more in the flower than he sees. I can imagine the cells inside, which also have a beauty. There's beauty not just at the dimension of one centimeter; there's also beauty at a smaller dimension.

There are the complicated actions of the cells, and other processes. The fact that the colors in the flower have evolved in order to attract insects to pollinate it is interesting; that adds a question: does this aesthetic sense we have also exist in lower forms of life? There are all kinds of interesting questions that come from knowledge of science, which only adds to the excitement and mystery and awe of a flower. It only adds. I don't understand how it subtracts.[2]

I agree with Feynman. Understanding human behavior as a subject of scientific study can only add to our ability to get the most out of our lives and subsequently add meaning and enjoyment to the lives of all we meet. While it may not be easy, it is worthwhile.

R⁺ MEMO   No. 4

Taking a systematic, data-based approach to

behavior can teach you a lot about life.

Signed _____

---

5 RELEARNING YOUR ABCs

Many receive advice; few profit from it.

—Publius Syrus (circa 42 bc)

Why do people do what they do? As we've mentioned, most people are obsessed with this question and look for the answers in all the wrong places, including the unreliable realm of common sense. But most often we look to a person's immediate or remote past. Of course, since precipitating events occur in the past, not in the present, the best we can do is speculate about what that event was, and this typically leads to nothing but unverifiable speculation.

This kind of analysis leads us to try to diagnose or psychoanalyze others. We constantly try to figure people out, interpret their behavior, understand or uncover their real motives, look into their past to find events that warped their personalities, or try to recall what "sets them off." This kind of activity, although interesting, is rarely accurate, and even more rarely is it productive.

"TELLING" ONLY GOES SO FAR

Most people think that changing behavior requires readiness on the part of the person in question. Therefore, the most common way people try to influence the behavior of others is to try to convince them of the need to change. Convincing comes in many forms but usually boils down to some form of telling others about their need to change, telling them what to change, telling them how to change, and telling them the consequences of changing or not changing. We suggest, educate, persuade, communicate, advise, beg, plead, counsel, and warn. In spite of all this, everybody probably remembers hearing the complaint, "If I've told you once, I've told you a thousand times." You may have said this a few times yourself. Every parent has said at one time or another, "I can't tell them anything anymore. They don't listen to a thing I say." Whether parent, supervisor, or spouse, we all know that telling usually has very little long-term impact.

Nonetheless, this society seems obsessed with telling. Labels on cigarette packs warn smokers of the dangers of smoking, yet millions continue to do so. Pregnant women are warned not to drink or use drugs, but thousands of babies are born every year with alcohol fetal syndrome or a drug addiction. Motorists are warned not to speed, but most do. Could the problem be that they did not see the warning or know the dangers involved? Hardly.

When we tell people to change and they don't, we usually resort to telling them again, but the second time we tell them more frequently or with more intensity. It has been said that the sole purpose of a child's middle name is to let the child know that he or she is in trouble. When your mother used your full name to call you, you knew it was not the first time she had called you.

The fact that people do not take all their prescribed medicine is estimated to cost $100 billion a year. A governmental task force studying the problem recommended that physicians *stress* to patients the importance of taking *all* their medicine. Most people have been given this advice but still have a cabinet stocked with partially finished prescriptions.

Stressing the point, warning that this is the last time you are going to tell them, telling them in no uncertain terms, retraining, and reminding are just other ways of trying the same thing harder. If telling one time doesn't work, the strategy most people use is to "tell them again."

Why do so many people think that telling is the best way to change behavior? One reason is that telling sometimes produces a temporary change. But while it may work on a limited basis, telling is not reliable or efficient in terms of long-term, meaningful behavior change. Another reason for resorting to telling is that people don't know what else to do when they want to change someone's behavior. The following explanation of the dynamics of human behavior will begin to give you a new, powerful tool you can use the next time you want to change the behavior of someone in your life.

TWO FACTORS INFLUENCE BEHAVIOR: THE ABC MODEL

There are two factors that influence behavior. One is what happens *before* a behavior occurs; the other is what happens *after* it occurs.

The technical name for actions or events that occur before a behavior and set the stage for it to occur is *antecedent*. Generally speaking, antecedents don't *cause* a behavior to occur. What causes behavior to occur are *consequences*. Consequences are events that are produced by behavior and occur during or after a behavior occurs. *If the behavior produces a consequence that the person wants or allows the person to avoid something he or she doesn't want, the behavior is more likely to occur again the next time the antecedent is present. If it does not, then the behavior most likely will not happen again.*

Here is a simple example to illustrate this point. We all have favorite restaurants. We were prompted to try them the first time by antecedents: a recommendation from a friend, an attractive sign or inviting outdoor seating, or perhaps a mouth-watering aroma when we walked by. These are the kinds of things that get a person to try a restaurant the first time. But it is what happened once you were in the restaurant, the consequences, which made you go back again. Those consequences may have included excellent service, wonderful food, or reasonable prices. The point is that it is always consequences that cause behavior to happen and recur.[1]

The figure below shows the ABC model of the dynamics of behavior change.

$$A: B \rightarrow C$$

A stands for "antecedent." The colon stands for "sets the stage." B stands for "behavior." The arrow points to the cause of behavior, C, the "consequence."

THE ABC GAME

This is a story most people can relate to. My daughter, age 7 at the time, is sitting in front of the TV. When I notice that it is past her bedtime, I say in a very fatherly voice, "Laura-Lee, honey, it is past your bedtime. Now you need to get up right now and go to bed." She replies with a resigned "Okay."

> A ("Laura-Lee, honey, it is past your bedtime."):
>
> B (Laura-Lee responds, "Okay.") →
>
> C (I leave. She continues to watch TV.)

I go about my business, thinking the situation has been handled. However, I pass the den a few minutes later, and there she sits. This time I say, "Young lady, I'm not going to tell you again. I want you to get up right now and go to bed." She moves as if to leave. Problem solved?

A ("Young lady, blah, blah, blah."):

B (She moves slightly.) →

C (I leave. She continues to watch TV.)

A few minutes later I'm back again, and I can't believe it. She is still there. Angrily, I say, "I'm *not* going to tell you again!" "I know, that's what you said last time," she replies. "Well, I *mean it* this time. Now, you better get in that bed!" She stands up and starts to leave. Thinking I have surely solved the problem this time, I leave only to return shortly to find her sitting back down! I shout, "Laura-Lee Daniels!" She immediately gets up and goes to bed.

Why did she get up when I used her full name and not before? The reason is very simple. In her experience, hearing her full name (antecedent) is highly correlated with action on my part (consequence). When she heard, "Laura-Lee, honey," she knew that she probably had another 30 minutes before I got angry. If "Laura-Lee Daniels!" is always followed by action on my part, it will always get action on her part. It's safe to say that Laura-Lee Daniels knew how to play the ABC game— and I don't mean reciting the alphabet!

Another interesting phenomenon is illustrated here. When I finally yelled (my behavior), she went to bed (desirable consequence for me). Her action at that point actually increased the probability that I would yell at her in the future. However, if when I said, "Laura-Lee, honey," I had taken her by the hand and made sure she went promptly to bed, I would have produced compliance, particularly if I positively reinforced complying frequently.

The same principles are sorely evident in the workplace. Most people at work can relate to the following story. Early one morning I was going to see a first-shift supervisor to talk to him about using positive reinforcement to solve a quality problem. As I approached the work area, his manager was vigorously poking him in the chest with his index finger. His face was red; his voice was loud; and his language was abusive. I was embarrassed and stood off to the side looking at my shoes. When the manager left, I walked up and said something like, "Boy! He's off to a rough start this morning." The supervisor said, "Aw, don't pay him no mind. That's the way he is. If I had been fired every time he told me I was going to be fired, I'd have been gone long ago. He threatens to fire me at least once a week!" What this man was telling me in effect was that the antecedent (yelling by the boss) was never associated with a consequence (firing the supervisor), and so it had no effect on the supervisor's performance.

A parent once asked me, "Why do I have to tell my children three times before they do what I ask?" "Because you tell them three times," I replied. If all that happens when you ask the first time is that you tell them again, the words come to have little meaning. The third time is the signal for action. However if you tell them one time and then make certain they do what you ask without further comment, they will soon respond the first time.

Antecedents become effective at producing desired behavior only *when they are a signal for a predictable consequence.* The most productive question you could ask in regard to changing behavior is, "What happens when they do that?" In other words, rather than looking at what triggered the behavior, you should look at the consequence, or what happened *after* the behavior. The consequence will tell you why a behavior is or is not occurring.

BEHAVIOR IS A FUNCTION OF ITS CONSEQUENCES

Consequences occur for every behavior. A behavioral consequence is an event produced by a behavior that affects the probability that the behavior will occur again. Therefore, behavioral consequences affect behavior in one of two ways: They either strengthen a behavior (increase its probability) or weaken it (decrease its probability). The way to know that a behavior has been strengthened or weakened is to note how often it occurs. If a behavior occurs more often than usual, it is being strengthened by its consequences. If it occurs less often than usual, it is being weakened by its consequences. This strengthening and weakening of behaviors is a continuous process. It happens to everybody—all the time.

Every time you do something, there is a consequence that affects that behavior in the future. That means you are changed every day of your life. The poets knew this. As Lord Byron said in *Childe Harold's Pilgrimage,* "I am not now that which I have been." Tennyson reiterated it in *Ulysses* when he wrote, "I am a part of all I have met."

We are constantly changing, and we change all those we meet. We provide consequences to the behavior of others, and they to ours. Every consequence we experience as a result of our behavior changes that behavior to some degree. Most of the time the change is so slight that we don't even notice it, but it is occurring nevertheless. It is a continuous process. You have no doubt heard it said or said yourself, "You are driving me crazy!" It is true. People drive each other crazy. More important, they also drive each other sane. In other words, we are a party to either maintaining or changing all the relationships we are involved in at work and elsewhere by the consequences we provide and receive.

Everybody knows that behaviors have consequences. We talk about them all the time in a casual way: "You had better not do that. She will be angry." "He will love it if you help." "If you do it this way, it will be easier." "You will hurt yourself if you keep doing that." "If you go, I'll never speak to you again." The list goes on and on.

Behavioral consequences are such a natural part of the environment that the average person doesn't think about them, and most people do not understand the precise way in which they affect behavior. However, when you see this, it makes it easier to understand why people do the things they do. More important, it makes it easier to bring about changes in the behavior of those you relate to at work, at home, and at play.

While most people think of consequences as negative, behavioral consequences can be positive or negative. When you get consequences, your behavior changes. When you don't get them, your behavior changes. Everyone understands if you touch a live wire and get shocked, it decreases the probability that you will touch it again. However, most people don't think about the fact that if you tell a joke and no one laughs, the absence of laughter (nothing happening) decreases the probability that you will tell another joke to that person or group.

Behavioral consequences include things as unobservable as what you say to yourself, as common as money, and as simple as a smile. A pat on the back, a note on one's performance, a thank you, an offer to help, and feedback on one's accomplishments can all have a positive and dramatic impact on performance and morale under the right circumstances. Under the wrong circumstances, these things can have the opposite effect. In later chapters I will detail the "right circumstances."

THE FOUR BEHAVIORAL CONSEQUENCES

For now let us turn our attention to the four basic behavioral consequences: what they are and how they work. They are

1. Positive reinforcers
2. Negative reinforcers
3. Punishers
4. Penalties

Each of these consequences has a distinct and predictable effect on behavior. Two of them—positive and negative reinforcers—increase behavior, and two—punishers and penalties—decrease it. In other words, if you want more of a behavior, you can use either positive or negative reinforcers. If you want less of a behavior, you can use punishers or penalties.

It should be noted that three of the four affect the performer negatively. Only positive reinforcement affects the performer positively. However, all are useful. In the popular press positive reinforcers have been presented as the consequence of choice to the extent that many people have the idea that they should always be used. My friends constantly ask me as they point to an inappropriate social behavior, "How can you positively reinforce that?" They assume that because of my work, I think that positive reinforcement is the only appropriate consequence. A very large percent of the population thinks likewise. Books such as *The Power of Positive Thinking* and *How to Win Friends and Influence People* have contributed to this mistaken belief. There is a time to use positive reinforcement as well as a time to use the other three consequences. The trick is knowing which one to deliver when and recognizing that you may be delivering the wrong one inadvertently, as the following story shows.

When I was being trained as a therapist, my supervisor and fellow interns sat behind a two-way mirror during group sessions, watching the patients as I interacted with them. There was a female patient in one particular group who talked incessantly, monopolizing the session.

After one of the sessions, as we were reviewing what went on, I complained to my professor, "Nate, what am I going to do about Mrs. B?" He looked at me with a straight face and said, "What do you mean?" I replied, "It should be obvious. She dominates the session. No one else has a chance to talk." Quizzically he asked, "You mean you don't want her to talk?" I got a little provoked by the question and responded, "Of course I don't. That should be obvious to anyone." He said, "I don't think it is to her. How could she know she is talking too much? When she talks, you look at her, you nod, you smile. You even occasionally ask her questions. Other members of the group do the same. Which of these things tell her that she is talking too much?"

I realized that I had been an unwitting party to the very behavior I was complaining about. As long as she continued to receive those positive consequences from me, she would continue to dominate the session. When I changed the consequences for her talking, the talking changed.

Since most people are unaware of the effect of consequences on behavior, it is not surprising that behaviors often receive unintended or inappropriate consequences. Even while in training as a therapist, I was unaware of the consequences I was delivering and repeatedly reinforcing behaviors I wanted to decrease. In other words, because we don't understand the nature of consequences, behavior that we want to occur less often frequently receives a consequence that strengthens it and behavior that we want to occur more often frequently receives consequences that weaken it.

TRUST AND DEPENDABILITY

A good example of the antecedent-consequence relationship is commonly called trust. The fact is that building trust is a simple matter. All you have to do to increase trust is to do (consequence to the other person) what you say you are going to do (antecedent). People who have a high correlation between what they say and what they do are trusted. People who don't are not.

A problem many people have in business is that they say things they cannot do or have no intention of doing. For example, a supervisor may say, "If you work hard and produce for me, I'll see that you get a promotion (antecedent)." After you work many long overtime hours and give the job your utmost effort, you are told that there is a freeze on promotions. There is no delivery of the promised reward (consequence to the performer). The fact that it may be out of the control of the supervisor does not change the fact that you have already done your part and that what was promised is not forthcoming. The result is that the supervisor is trusted less and management as a whole is trusted less. In the terms of behavior analysis, the antecedent was not reliably paired with the promised consequence.

Most people would be trusted and respected more if they said less and did more. Jesse, "the Body," Ventura, a former professional wrestler, shocked the country by being elected governor of Minnesota. He made no promises to the voters because he said he didn't know what he would be able to do as governor. All he said was that he would do his best. This was unprecedented in modern politics. It was a novel enough antecedent that the voters decided to give him a chance. Trust and respect are earned through action (consequence), not through promises (antecedent).

MODELING

Another form of antecedent is what is known as modeling. People tend to copy the behavior of those they see being reinforced in ways they would like to be reinforced. A teenager who is picked on may model the language, dress, and habits of a movie star he sees as being successful in dealing with such problems. Another who wants to be popular may imitate the behavior of someone she knows who is popular. It could be a celebrity, older sibling, parent, relative, teacher, or friend.

Modeling the behavior of others is very common among children but occurs at all ages. Sports heroes, movie stars, rock stars, business moguls, and beautiful young people in slick advertisements all serve as antecedents for the behavior of the spectators and media watchers who are caught up in the current of the common culture. The bad news is that while modeling is very powerful, it is not always a positive force. One has only to look at gang culture to see how potent modeling is within groups that behave in such antisocial ways.

Phil Hurst, an Aubrey Daniels International (ADI) consultant, describes an incident in which a manager who was frequently given to fits of temper chewed out an employee one day for no apparent reason. An employee who witnessed it commented, "I see you got a 'drive-by shooting.'" As strange as it may sound, a "drive-by shooting" became a positive reinforcer. People wanted to know, "Who got the drive-by shooting today?" They began to imitate the behaviors of fellow employees who got chewed out from this manager. Of course, this practice of the manager was totally ineffective in producing the performance he wanted.

No matter how powerful modeling is in prompting behavior, it is still the consequence that gets the behavior to recur. An important lesson in the science of human behavior is that the antecedent of modeling, coupled with reliable consequences that are valuable to the person, is a potent tool in producing behavioral change.

ONLY TWO PROBLEMS IN PSYCHOLOGY

As I was leaving graduate school, ready to make my mark on the world, I had to drop off some final paperwork in the psychology department's office. I ran into one of my professors, Dr. Cohen, who wanted to philosophize. In the conversation he pronounced, "Well, you know, there are really only two problems in psychology." My reaction was, "I've been here 5 years and now you tell me there are only two problems in psychology!" "That's right," he replied. "What are they?" I asked because I honestly didn't know. "The first," he said, "is how to get a behavior to occur one time. The second is how to get it to occur again."

Antecedents set the stage for a behavior to occur one time. Consequences get it to occur again and again.

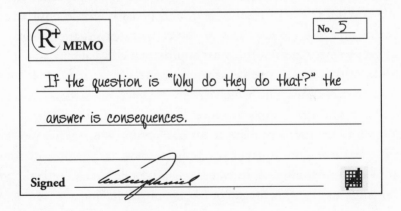

MEMO No. 5

If the question is "Why do they do that?" the answer is consequences.

Signed

6 THE OTHER THREE CONSEQUENCES

"Always be positive" is the worst advice you
could ever give or receive.

—A. Daniels

To appreciate fully the power of positive reinforcement, it is necessary to understand the other three consequences: negative reinforcement, punishment, and penalty. While positive reinforcement is the consequence of choice in most situations, there are occasions where it is not the most appropriate consequence to use. You will learn that these three negative consequences are indicated in some circumstances, but that they never solve a problem by themselves; they only buy you time. Only positive reinforcement offers a permanent solution to the problem of behavior change. At best negative reinforcement, punishment, and penalty only get you in position to solve a problem. Surprisingly, of the three, negative reinforcement is the most frequently used consequence for influencing behavior.

NEGATIVE REINFORCEMENT: ONCE ON SHORE, WE PRAY NO MORE

Negative reinforcement generates behavior that is directed toward avoiding or escaping punishment. Negative reinforcement is effective.

That means you can get behavior to occur and even increase by using negative reinforcement. Since negative reinforcement gets things done, why should you worry about using positive reinforcement? There are several reasons, and one of the more important is that with negative reinforcement, people perform only to the level necessary to avoid some kind of unpleasantness. They never reach optimum levels of performance or give all of their discretionary effort. Negative reinforcement, when used to influence behavior, is really a matter of managing through the use of threat or fear. The threat may be overt or implied. It may be as overt as "Do this or you will be fired" or as subtle as the fear that if you don't do something, you won't be liked or will disappoint someone. Peer pressure is a common form of negative reinforcement. Negative reinforcement is part of the "do it or else" school of thought, which produces compliance but unfortunately also produces an environment filled with frowns, hard feelings, and lackluster performance.

The sad truth about negative reinforcement is that it dominates a great many people's lives. Many people spend the majority of their lives doing things because they "have to." Most children do their homework because they have to. Most people go to work because they have to. Most people pay their taxes because they have to.

There are many other things we do because we have to. We don't think much about them, but we still do them because of negative reinforcement. For example, most people do not go to the dentist because they want to; they go because they are afraid of what will happen if they don't. Indeed, some people put it off until the pain of a bad tooth is unbearable and finally go to the dentist to escape the pain. Most people feel an obligation to pay taxes, but you know it is negatively reinforcing because it is safe to say that no one pays more taxes than are due and most people wait to file until the last minute unless they are expecting a refund. There are numerous things we do every day where the minimum response is enough. We stop at a stoplight, and that is all that is needed. We don't want people to do more than that. Stopping before you get to the light is certainly not helpful, and remaining stopped after the light turns green will get you in trouble with the others waiting at the light.

Thus, if you want only a mimimum response, negative reinforcement will work. However, there is another feature of negative reinforcement of which you should be aware. *A behavior controlled by negative reinforcers will stop when the fear or threat of punishment is removed.* Taking medicine is a good example. As we discussed in Chapter 5, many people abandon their medicine early, skip doses, or don't get their prescriptions filled—traits that keep them sick and have contributed to a surge in drug-resistant diseases. The reason is easy to understand. Taking medicine is a behavior managed by negative reinforcers. When the pain or other symptoms go away, taking medicine stops even though the illness may not have been cured.

It has been said in business many times, "I don't care if they like it. I just want them to do it." This kind of management is expensive because it requires increased supervision or dependence on rules and policies.

Some parents have been shocked at reports of their children's behavior when the children have left home after they have graduated from high school. When college or work officials confront the parents with their kids' misbehavior, the parents can't believe it. They say, "That couldn't be my child. He always behaved at home. He never did anything like that." Frequently what has happened, of course, is that the child behaved the way he did at home because he was afraid of what would happen if he didn't. When he was away from the threat of punishment, he began to do things he would have liked to do at home but did not do because punishment was imminent. The "good behavior" the parents witnessed at home was motivated by negative reinforcement because that behavior was controlled by the avoidance of punishment.

Stress at work is rarely caused by the work itself but results primarily from performing under negative reinforcement, punishment, or penalty conditions. If you want to decrease stress, quit using negative reinforcement and punishment to manage people. Positive reinforcement is the best antidote for stress. Jobs don't stress people unless they are too hot, too cold, too physically demanding, or confining. People are by far the greatest cause of stress at work. High activity rates and deadlines energize people in one company and stress them out in others. In hospital emergency rooms I have seen the staff stressed out and burned out. When you talk to them, they don't talk about the job functions; they talk about management or coworkers who perform poorly. You can go to another emergency room across town with a similar patient population and find a group of people who are excited about the large number of people they serve in a day and the quality medical care the hospital gives. What makes the difference is not the job; *it's what happens to them when they do the job.* One emergency room is managed by negative reinforcement, and the other by positive reinforcement. Negative reinforcement, punishment, and penalty in the workplace produce stress.

Since negative reinforcement occurs when you escape or avoid something, all you have to do to create negative reinforcement is provide a situation in which people will work to avoid a consequence they don't want. You just need to frighten people from time to time. It doesn't take much effort to use guilt, duty, obligation, or fear of disapproval to get things done, but remember that there is a hidden cost to these methods. The cost is counted in terms of poor to mediocre performance at home, at work, and at school and by stressful relationships in all those places. You will never capture a person's spirit or heart with negative reinforcement. That requires positive reinforcement. A Greek philosopher said it well: "Change a man against his will, he's of the same opinion still."

PUNISHMENT: STOP THAT!

As a parent and as a boss, with strangers and with friends, I have found that punishing is very difficult for me to do. However, I realize that there are occasions when if I care for the person, I must do something to stop behavior that is detrimental to that person in the long run even though it may involve some short-term loss of positive reinforcement for them and me. Not doing something to stop inappropriate behavior is a way of saying, "I don't care about your long-term happiness." Dr. Laura Schlessinger of talk radio fame says that a parent who supports a child when the child is wrong is a "rotten parent." I certainly agree. Likewise, a manager who supports a supervisor when she is wrong is a rotten manager. A union steward who supports a union member when he is wrong is a rotten steward. A coach who supports a player who is wrong is a rotten coach. Unfortunately, too many examples appear daily in newspapers, magazines, and television where this is the case. There are occasions when letting your children experience the negative consequences of their behavior is the best thing you can do to support their long term adjustment. It is often the best thing you can do in other relationships as well.

It is important to keep in mind that the word *punish* as it is used here has a different meaning than it does in the vernacular. To *punish*, as defined by Webster, is "to impose a penalty as pain, suffering, shame, strict restraint, or loss upon someone for some fault, offense or violation." In other words, the common use of the word implies action on the part of the one doing the punishing. In the context of this book, the term *punishment* is used to describe any behavioral consequence delivered after a behavior that reduces its frequency. While pain, suffering, shame, restraint, and loss can reduce behavior under some circumstances, the behavioral definition goes beyond those concepts.

For example, an incident happened in our office a while back. We publish a quarterly magazine in-house. We used to have the covers designed by an outside company, but at the suggestion of Sandy and Tracy, two members of the administrative staff, we brought this task into the office to reduce costs. Sandy came to me one day all excited, held up the rough draft of the first cover Tracy had produced, and said, "Whatta you think, Doc?" I paused because my eye caught a small detail I didn't like. I actually liked the overall effect of the cover, but before I said that I liked it, Sandy said, "You don't like it." I protested, "No, I like it." "No, I can tell you don't," she replied.

At that point, no matter what I said, it seemed to make things worse. Sandy felt punished. The excitement in her eyes vanished, and her smile turned into a concerned expression. The enthusiasm she had felt for the project evaporated right before my eyes. It was obvious that my response was a punisher for Sandy. I'm sure when Sandy related the event to Tracy, her enthusiasm for the task was dampened as well. Don't misunderstand me. This was not a big thing. It did not materially affect the quality of the magazine or do significant harm to our relationships. However, it was punishing because it did have a depressing effect on their performance, at least in the short run. If you do a small thing like this many times a day, it can have a material effect on attitude and performance. Inadvertent punishment is much more common in daily affairs than is intentional punishment.

Because of the many difficulties associated with punishment, it should be used only as a last resort. To quote Sophocles, punishment can turn out to be "a remedy too strong for the disease."[1] The following are some of the many problems associated with the use of punishment.

PUNISHING AN UNDESIRABLE BEHAVIOR DOESN'T GUARANTEE THAT A DESIRABLE ONE WILL TAKE ITS PLACE

At best punishment stops problem behavior. Just stopping a behavior solves few problems because if you are not doing one thing, you are doing another. Therefore, stopping one behavior will cause another behavior to take its place. For example, if you spend an hour a day engaging in a bad habit and you stop it, what will you do during that time? Someone who smokes a pack of cigarettes a day will spend at least 2 hours directly and indirectly smoking or preparing to smoke. Two hours is a lot of time for which to find a substitute behavior. I have gone on fasts from time to time, and my biggest problem was finding something to do when others were eating. I came to realize that people spend a lot of time involved in behaviors related to eating.

Because there are practically always more ways to do something wrong than to do it right, by punishing the wrong behavior without reinforcing a constructive alternative, you are likely to get another problem behavior. A child who has been caught smoking will make sure that no parent or teacher is around when she has another cigarette and will go to great lengths to hide the pack and disguise the smell of smoke in the future.

I have known managers who punished someone in the office for making excessive personal telephone calls only to discover that when the personal calls stopped, the person spent that time talking to other employees about personal matters. This was worse than the original problem because now the person not only was not doing his work but also was interrupting the work of others. An employee who has been reprimanded for taking a shortcut through a restricted area may look around to make sure no one sees her before taking the shortcut again. When you punish one behavior, you need to positively reinforce a *constructive* alternative.

THE BEHAVIOR THAT GETS PUNISHED MAY NOT BE THE BEHAVIOR YOU WANT TO STOP

When people's behavior has been punished, they are motivated to avoid the punishment in the future. It is not uncommon for a parent to punish a child for excessive or loud talking in public only to discover that the child now won't talk in the presence of adults. An employee who is punished for making what the boss calls "a stupid comment" may make no more comments of any kind. Someone who embarrasses a person in public may find that that person avoids all contact with him or her in the future. The fact that punishing one behavior may generalize to other similar behaviors makes punishment tricky to use effectively.

PUNISHMENT, LIKE POSITIVE REINFORCEMENT, IS HIGHLY INDIVIDUAL

It is difficult to determine what is punishing. Arguing, while punishing to some, may be highly reinforcing to others. A common form of attempted punishment in the workplace is to "chew someone out." I know many situations in which a chewing out is a form of attention which can be highly reinforcing for some people.

Dr. Tom Connellan, a behavior analyst who consulted with a juvenile detention center years ago, reported a classic example of this. The staff presented him with the problem of frequent vandalism in the center. The boys would write graffiti on the walls, stop up the commodes, rip the sinks off the walls, and engage in other negative acts too numerous to mention and impossible for the average adult to imagine. Since these were behaviors that needed to be stopped, the first thing the staff thought of was how to punish the boys; not an entirely inappropriate solution.

They had brainstormed things they thought would be punishing to the boys. One staff member suggested putting anyone caught vandalizing the jail on a diet of bread and water for a number of days. They thought that because teenage boys liked to eat so much, this would be punishing. Believe it or not, the number of acts of vandalism increased.

Dr. Connellan had taught the staff that an increase in behavior indicates a reinforcer. How could a diet of bread and water be a reinforcer? Look at it this way. The thing that most of these kids had in common was failure. Their days were filled with conversations like the following: "You think you're bad? You don't know bad. Let me tell you bad." Then they would relate something they had done that was more illegal, immoral, or antisocial than what they had just heard. Being put on bread and water was just something else to brag about: "Let me tell you bad. One time I spent 10 days on nothin' but bread and water!"

Dr. Connellan suggested that rather than putting them on bread and water, the staff should put them on baby food. Get the picture? "You think you're bad. Let me tell you bad. I spent 10 days on baby food!" Doesn't sound bad or macho, does it? It certainly wasn't something they wanted to brag about. The vandalism quickly stopped.

THE BEHAVIOR OF PUNISHING OFTEN PROVIDES POSITIVE REINFORCEMENT FOR THE ONE DOING THE PUNISHING

Because punishment often gets an immediate response from the person being punished, it provides positive reinforcement for the person doing the punishing. For instance, if someone is doing something you don't like and you politely ask him or her to stop, that person may continue for a while before stopping. However, if you yell, "Stop it *now!*" chances are that he or she will stop immediately. Remember, any behavior that gets you what you want immediately is very reinforcing to you. This explains the behavior of bullies and those who engage in domestic abuse. It is common in the workplace for managers and supervisors who yell and scream to get quick change in the behavior of those who are "yelled at," and that perpetuates the yelling and screaming. This is certainly one of the reasons punishment is as common as it is in this society.

There are other problems with punishment as a way to change behavior, but these are enough to show you that it is difficult to use effectively. The best way to avoid these problems is to focus on positively reinforcing behavior that is incompatible with the behavior you don't want. If punishment is indicated, be sure to positively reinforce immediately any change for the better.

PENALTY

Penalty is often difficult to distinguish from punishment, and in many situations the distinction is unimportant because they both reduce behavior. However, there is at least one difference that has practical consequences which are important in everyday life. Penalty occurs when you lose something you have that you care about. There are many examples of this in family life. Siblings who are watching TV start fighting, and you turn the TV off. A child misbehaves, and you take his allowance from him. You "ground" a teenager. A girl breaks a date because of something stupid her boyfriend said or did.

The law uses penalty as a primary way to stop behavior. Sanctions operate as behavioral penalties. Fines are common for minor violations of the law, and depriving people of their freedom is used for more serious violations. In all these situations, your behavior causes something to be taken from you.

NOTHING MORE TO LOSE

Penalty has all the drawbacks of punishment. However, there is an additional aspect of penalty that you should be aware of before using it. Because you are losing what you have, what happens when you have nothing more to lose? We see this when criminals have committed murders that result in the death penalty. Committing more murders will not result in their losing more! At that point penalty not only is ineffective but may set up "going out in a blaze of glory" as a positive reinforcer. Solitary confinement is an extreme penalty. It is not unusal for prisoners isolated to continue to do outrageous things because in a perverse way they are in control and the officials are powerless to increase the penalty.

Almost all parents have experienced this effect of penalty, albeit to a much lesser degree. If you have ever told a teenager that he or she has been "grounded" for a period of time and had the teenager respond, "I don't care," you can relate to the problem of using penalty as a means of stopping an undesirable behavior. I have known parents who become increasingly frustrated as they restrict, deprive, and limit the activities of their children only to have the children continue to do things that cause the parents to impose more penalties. If you stand back and take a dispassionate view of such situations, you can see that the child is using countercontrol methods on the parents. While the parents think they are in control, the child is the one who is causing the parents to act.

Does this mean that penalties should not be used? Absolutely not. Often brief restrictions or light fines will solve a behavior or performance problem. However, if you find yourself using penalties more and more, you are probably in a counterproductive situation.

Now that you have a fundamental understanding of negative reinforcers, punishers, and penalties, at least three things should be clear. First, they are involved in all normal interactions, at least over time. Second, they are difficult to use effectively. Third, they never solve a problem by themselves. If they work to stop an undesirable behavior, the most effective way to move forward is to find a desirable alternative to positively reinforce.

The best and most lasting solution to behavior problems is positive reinforcement. It is the most powerful, efficient, and effective way to change and influence human behavior. The rest of this book details its use.

R⁺ MEMO	No. _6_

Negative consequences never solve a problem

by themselves.

Signed _Audrey Daniel_

7 THE NATURE OF POSITIVE REINFORCEMENT
How Positive Reinforcement Sustains Behavior

I can live for two months on a good compliment.

—MARK TWAIN

BEHAVIOR GOES WHERE REINFORCEMENT FLOWS

Positive reinforcement is the most effective way to change any behavior—your own or someone else's. It is the most desirable consequence to use to change behavior, and for many reasons. It doesn't cost anything, and so you don't need a budget to use it. You don't need authority or permission to put it into action. People enjoy receiving it, and it gives the best results on a continuing basis, producing cooperation, creativity, and high productivity. It is effective, easy to use, and fun to give and receive. It's also the consequence of choice because it changes behavior with less risk of creating anger, hard feelings, and negative fallout. In short, of all the behavior change processes, positive reinforcement is the most powerful, the most desirable, and the least risky.

POSITIVE REINFORCEMENT DEFINED

A positive reinforcer is any consequence that follows a behavior and results in an increase in that behavior. Positive reinforcement is the procedure of delivering a positive reinforcer. These are technical definitions; to use positive reinforcement efficiently and effectively, it is important to understand these concepts in this way.

When you understand positive reinforcement in this way, you realize that common practices such as a pat on the back, an atta-boy, an annual bonus, and an employee-of-the-month award do not necessarily qualify as positive reinforcers. While a compliment was obviously a positive reinforcer for Mark Twain's behavior and for that of many others, it is not for everyone. *What you do to someone does not define positive reinforcement; it is defined by what happens to the person's behavior after you do it.*

Positive reinforcement always works. That is, it always increases behavior. If the behavior does not increase after an attempt at reinforcement, the attempt wasn't a reinforcer or wasn't delivered correctly.

POSITIVE REINFORCEMENT IS EVERYWHERE

Positive reinforcement occurs every time you do something that produces an effect in your environment that you like. When it is defined in this way, you can see that everybody gets thousands of positive reinforcers every day. The TV coming on positively reinforces pushing the power button on the remote control. Receiving a candy bar positively reinforces putting money in a vending machine and pushing a button. Hitting a golf ball is reinforced by seeing it land on the green close to the hole.

POSITIVE REINFORCEMENT EQUALS "EASY" AND "USER-FRIENDLY"

Things that are easy to do are more reinforcing than are things that are hard to do. The concept of being "user-friendly" is really the process of building positive reinforcers into using a computer or another device.

For instance, every time you move successfully from one program to another, the commands you use that get you where you want to go provide you with positive reinforcement. Computer games are designed to produce many positive reinforcers per minute. Every time a player pushes a button and the characters move in the desired direction, the player gets reinforced. In most computer games this kind of reinforcement can occur at a rate of more than 100 per minute! This is why people become so engrossed in playing these games. New versions of the games are successful when they produce more reinforcers than the old ones do. Keep in mind that positive reinforcers are not limited to what people say and do to others. Most reinforcement results from normal interaction with our environment.

GOOD INTENTIONS ARE NOT ENOUGH

Positive reinforcement can unintentionally increase an undesired behavior just as it increases a desired behavior. Have you ever been in a situation where the harder you tried to solve a problem, the worse it got? If "worse" means that the negative behavior is occurring more often, the things you were doing to solve the problem were actually positive reinforcers for the undesired behavior. For example, it has been demonstrated many times in elementary classrooms that the more times a teacher tells some students to sit down, the more they stand up. What this should indicate to the teacher is that saying "Sit down" is actually a positive reinforcer for standing up. Having the teacher spend time with the children who are seated while ignoring those who are standing until they are seated typically solves the problem. Spending time with the "misbehaving" students once they are doing work at their desks will maintain the desirable behavior.

In my clinical practice I saw a young female patient who had started pulling out her eyelashes and eyebrows. The problem got so bad that she had practically no eyebrows or eyelashes left. When her parents would see her pulling on her lashes or eyebrows, they would tell her to stop it. I had them collect some data on their behavior, and they discovered to their amazement that saying "Stop it" was actually a reinforcer for pulling out her lashes and eyebrows. The more they said "Stop it," the more she pulled out her eyelashes and eyebrows. The attention her parents gave to the undesired behavior actually reinforced it, and so it increased.

Conversely, we sometimes do things we think are reinforcers and discover later that they were actually punishers. A supervisor in a label-making plant heard about how effective performance feedback was in improving performance and started giving feedback to performers daily. He would go up to them and tell them how many labels they had run the previous day. Fortunately, he kept data because the number of labels produced dropped dramatically. The supervisor could not understand that what he had done was negative. Maybe it was the abrupt way he gave the workers the information or the fact that they weren't used to having him communicate with them. Maybe they thought he was keeping track of their performance to get evidence for firing them. Whatever the reason, the performance data told him that his behavior was not positively reinforcing because the desirable behavior decreased.

DO UNTO OTHERS AS *THEY* WOULD HAVE YOU DO UNTO THEM

The concept that most people have of positive reinforcement is limited to what are called social and tangible reinforcers. While they constitute only a small proportion of the reinforcers a person gets every day, tangible and social reinforcers play a vital role in developing and maintaining effective habits.

Social and tangible reinforcers generally are defined as the things a person wants or likes. While this is not a scientific definition, it is useful in understanding and using the concept. This definition is broad enough to include making money, liking chocolate, wanting to please someone, and wanting to make someone angry. Probably the thing that differentiates one person from another more than anything else is that we all like and dislike different things. There are no two people, not even identical twins, who like exactly the same things all the time.

The best way to understand what another person really likes is to watch how that person spends his or her discretionary time and money. Looking only at what people *say* they like and value can often distract you from what they *really* value.

A good way to appreciate the infinite variety of positive reinforcers is to discover people's hobbies. There seems to be no end to what people will collect or spend free time doing. Think of all the things people hunt and collect. There is a group of people, a society, that collects "dated railroad nails." Imagine finding pleasure walking down old railroad tracks. As a man told me once, "I must have walked 500 miles of railroad tracks this year." He was eager to show me his collection and offered to give me a "starter set." You probably know people whose hobby is work. That results from the fact that they have received more reinforcement there than in any other place or activity.

BOREDOM EQUALS LACK OF POSITIVE REINFORCEMENT

What a person finds reinforcing has little to do with the behavior involved. Repetition has often been thought of as the problem in most jobs. Academics have chided business because many jobs are repetitious and boring. Boredom is not caused by repetition; it is caused by lack of positive reinforcement for repeated behaviors. The behaviors in most sports and other leisure activities are often very repetitious. Sewing, cooking, and gardening can all be said to be repetitious. However, that repetition leads to frequent reinforcers, and that is precisely why people enjoy them. Attempts to "enrich" jobs by changing what people do have not been effective. *It is not what people do that determines job satisfaction; it is what happens to them when they do it.*

During my college years I was a disc jockey in the summers and school holidays at a local radio station. I made more money on that job than I thought I would ever make as an adult. I had almost total control of how I ran the programs. But after only 2 years I became very disenchanted with the job. I remember thinking that I would tear my hair out if I had to read one more commercial about the price of bacon at Piggly Wiggly. I was bored. Yet I had a job that many people wanted.

Because I had no training for the job, I made many mistakes. Naturally, there were lots of negative consequences that undermined my self-confidence. Since I got few reinforcers for what I did right and lots of punishers for what I did wrong, I decided that I didn't really like that kind of job after all. By the way, I got lots of reinforcers from listeners. But because I was learning, my most important reinforcers were those from management, and I got very few. I realize now that if management had responded differently, I probably would have made a career in radio. As it was, I quit the job and changed my major to psychology.

I've seen people excited about their jobs in a research lab, and I've seen people bored with janitorial jobs. Conversely, I've seen people fired up about janitorial jobs and people bored with research jobs. I cannot think of a job that cannot be made into something that people hate to do. No matter what behaviors are involved in a job, increasing the frequency of positive reinforcement associated with those behaviors can increase the meaning and enjoyment of the job.

MEANING DOES NOT RESIDE IN BEHAVIOR; IT RESIDES IN CONSEQUENCES

While we might say that reading is a positive reinforcer to a particular person, turning the pages and looking at the words on a page are not the reinforcers. It is experiencing the suspense of a mystery, the romanticism of a love story, the adventure of learning about new places, or learning how and why things work that provides the actual reinforcement.

The game of golf is probably the best example of how meaning is not found in behavior and how the problem of boredom and meaningless work is not caused by repetition. Millions of people worldwide pay to do the same thing over and over every chance they get. I am personally crazy about the game. I hate cold weather, and the only thing I will voluntarily do in the cold is play golf. But what do I do when I play? Hit it and try to find it. Hit it and try to find it. Knock it in the hole and start all over again. If I live to be 90, I hope I will still be able to get out and do those things over and over again.

It is possible that some people reading this believe that golf is a waste of time. Golf is a stupid waste of time only to those who have never experienced the positive reinforcement associated with a long straight drive, a shot that lands within a foot of the hole, and the sight and sound of a long putt falling into the cup. In addition, I probably receive more social reinforcement in a round of golf than the average person receives at work in several months. Mark Twain stated it well: "There is probably no pleasure equal to the pleasure of climbing a dangerous Alp; but it is a pleasure which is confined strictly to people who find pleasure in it!"[1]

As with golf, the behaviors involved in the vast majority of hobbies are not dramatic or exotic. People who love golf are people who have received lots of reinforcement for hitting the ball and trying to find it. People who love needlework are people who have had a lot of reinforcement making hundreds of thousands of stitches. Any hobby is the same. A hobby is simply an activity for which the hobbyist receives a lot of positive reinforcement.

"I have never been to a professional baseball game or seen an episode of *Dallas, Geraldo,* or *Oprah,*" said the columnist William F. Buckley. "So I waste my time and find my pleasures in other ways." Find how people "waste their time" and you will have discovered what is reinforcing to them.

R+ KEEPS BEHAVIOR ALIVE

Positive reinforcement is the lifeblood of efficiency and effectiveness. Without it, behavior withers and dies. Sustaining behavior is simply a matter of making sure that it receives enough reinforcement to keep it going. If a behavior decreases over time, that probably has occurred because the amount of reinforcement is not sufficient to keep the behavior going at a high and steady rate. The technical term for the withdrawal or removal of positive reinforcement from a previously reinforced behavior is *extinction*. It is a very important concept in understanding how to sustain behavior, because a lot of the problems people experience at work and at home result from inadvertent extinction.

EXTINCTION—STOPPING BEHAVIOR BY DOING NOTHING

Extinction occurs when behavior that previously was reinforced is no longer reinforced. Extinction occurs every day. Behaviors that don't work for us, that is, don't get us what we want, eventually stop. Every day behaviors are strengthened and weakened. Behaviors that work are strengthened; those that don't are weakened. Extinction is a good thing because without it, we would still have every bad habit we ever had.

The problem with extinction is that the process is not directly observable. Since extinction is a passive process, you may not notice anything happening immediately, but, slowly you will see behavior changing. Every time you do something and nothing happens, that behavior is weakened.

This brings up two practical issues related to the use of extinction to eliminate undesirable behavior. One is making sure that behavior we want to continue is not extinguished accidentally, and the other is making sure that behavior we want to extinguish doesn't get reinforced accidentally. In the first situation we must make sure that behaviors which are desirable from a personal and societal point of view get at least some occasional reinforcement. When reinforcement becomes too infrequent, extinction will occur.

Deliberately removing or withholding reinforcement is difficult for most people to do. The most common example of deliberate extinction is ignoring. Ignoring, like breaking up, is hard to do. In the mental health facility where I worked as a young therapist, we taught the staff members how to ignore behavior because we discovered that while most of them thought they were ignoring, they weren't. When you ignore, it is as though the behavior was not happening or did not exist. You don't ignore by staring at someone or looking sternly with your hands on your hips. You simply go about your business as though it was not happening.

Since we have been reinforced all our lives for looking at people and listening to what they say, it is hard to selectively ignore. It may seem easy, but it is not. If you've ever said that someone has a way of "hitting my hot button." "getting on my nerves," or "getting under my skin," this usually means that that person has done something that can't be ignored. Anybody who has raised children understands this. Children won't be ignored. They are experts at getting their parents' attention whether the parents want to give it to them or not, and often they get it with inappropriate behavior such as crying, nagging, or anger.

Not only do parents have a hard time ignoring this type of negative behavior, our whole society does. If society could ignore weird, antisocial, counterproductive behavior, many of the problems that plague the world would soon disappear. Think about all the crazy things people do to get attention. Teenagers don't put earrings through their tongues because it feels good. If no one else knew it or saw it, would they do it? The truth is that for some people negative attention is better than no attention at all. The recent tragic shootings in several U.S. high schools can be attributed in part to a craving for attention. Dio Chrysostom, a Greek philosopher, said, "Most men are so completely corrupted by opinion that they would rather be notorious for the greatest calamities than suffer no ill and be unknown."[2]

In situations where behavior is undergoing extinction (not receiving the usual reinforcement) several things happen. The first is that the old behavior increases in an effort to get reinforcement. This is called an *extinction burst*. One might say that when a person is not getting reinforcement as he or she used to, that person tries harder. A child who gets his way by kicking and screaming may kick faster and scream louder when his parents begin to ignore it. Many parents make the mistake of thinking that ignoring the behavior isn't working because the behavior is getting worse. Actually, the opposite is true. The increase in the behavior tells the parents that the child is not getting reinforcement and is trying harder for it. Unfortunately, at this point many parents give in and respond to the child, which puts the behavior on intermittent reinforcement, increasing resistance to extinction in the future and making the behavior harder to eliminate. I've seen this happen in labor negotiations where management would not respond to labor's demands until there was violence, at which time it would find a way to settle.

The second thing you can expect after the onset of extinction is emotional behavior. This is the situation where you kick the vending machine, curse the company, or blame your spouse or where a child holds her breath and "turns blue." This is a natural response to the loss of reinforcement and should be expected. Grief is a response to the loss of reinforcement. The cure for grief is to find other sources of reinforcement. When a romantic relationship breaks up, the length of grief is directly related to how quickly the parties find other sources of reinforcement. The best thing you can do to help people in situations where they have lost a loved one through death or divorce is to get them to be active so that they are likely to find new sources of reinforcement.

One final aspect of extinction is called resurgence. *Resurgence* refers to a well-known phenomenon in which an old behavior disappears for a period of time and then, for no apparent reason, pops up again. Dr. Robert Epstein, a prominent behavioral researcher, discovered that this is basically the result of inadequate reinforcement for the new behavior.[3] I have had many people in my seminars come up to me and say, "My boss needs this positive reinforcement stuff." I have occasionally responded, "Bad news. Your boss has had this positive reinforcement stuff." "I know," comes the reply. "He was better when he first came back from the training, but now he is worse than ever." My response is, "You screwed up, didn't you?" What I go on to tell them is that when their boss attempted a new behavior he learned in a performance management workshop, he didn't get enough reinforcement to keep the new behavior going. Extinction set in, and he reverted to the most reinforced previous behavior. If the old way of behaving gets reinforced, it is inadvertently strengthened and will be more difficult to extinguish in the future. The lesson is that when you want to extinguish one behavior, you need to provide plenty of reinforcement for the new behavior that you want to take its place.

As with punishment, extinction rarely solves a behavior problem by itself. Thus, in attempting to use extinction, the positive reinforcement of a productive alternative behavior is critical. The following are some cautions about the use of extinction.

1. *Extinction is not appropriate when you cannot withhold all the reinforcement.* If you can ignore something but others won't, the best you can hope for is that the behavior will not occur in your presence. Many times this is all you want, but if you are concerned about the general welfare of the other person, unless you can get everybody to ignore the behavior, extinction will not produce the change you want.

2. *Extinction takes time.* Depending on the strength of the habit being extinguished, the amount of time it takes to eliminate the behavior will vary widely. It could take as little as a few hours, or it could take several weeks. If the behavior cannot be tolerated easily, choose another way to solve the problem. For example, if a behavior is dangerous, do not try extinction because someone could get hurt before extinction works. The appropriate consequence in that case would be punishment.

3. *Extinction is difficult to do.* Extinction requires patience and diligence. Once you decide to use extinction, you will create a more difficult problem if you lose your resolve before the undesired behavior is completely gone. If you don't have both patience and diligence, don't try this way of solving the problem.

Even though behavioral priniciples are simple to understand, they are hard to apply because when we apply reinforcement to the behavior of others, we cannot exempt ourselves from the process. If the behavior we use to try to change another person's behavior does not receive positive reinforcement, it will not be sustained. To avoid some of the pitfalls in the behavior change process, there are a number of other reinforcement rules that must be understood to apply the process effectively. You will learn about them in the next chapter.

R⁺ MEMO

No. 7

Only positive reinforcement brings out the best in people.

Signed _____

8 EVERYBODY THINKS THEY'RE DOING IT

Ingratitude is a crime so shameful that the man was never yet found who would acknowledge himself guilty of it

—OLD PROVERB

When I speak to managers across the country, it is not unusual for them to say, "I use positive reinforcement all the time." Yet when you ask their employees when they last received positive reinforcement from the boss, the most common answer by far is "I can't remember." How could this be? Is somebody lying? Probably not. The employees are right that if they don't feel they have been reinforced, they probably haven't been. However, the manager probably did make *attempts* to reinforce, but just because the manager intended somethings he said or did to be a reinforcer doesn't mean that it was. Because of this, many more people think they use positive reinforcement effectively than actually do.

Most people consider that they have a positive effect on others because their motives and intentions are positive. As you will discover, being positive and using positive reinforcement effectively are different things. For instance, the problems business faces in regard to safety, quality, productivity, and morale would not exist to the extent they do if positive reinforcement were being applied effectively. If teachers used positive reinforcement correctly to create more effective performance, the vast majority of students would be excelling. If families were using positive reinforcement effectively, children's behavior and family values would not be a national concern. The fact is that none of our institutions, very few of our leaders, and hardly any members of the general population understand how to use this powerful tool to influence human behavior in the most effective way.

Probably no one would disagree that given equal results, positive reinforcement is the preferred choice over negative approaches to problem solving. Given that fact, why do negative approaches appear to be the norm? In spite of all the things businesses have done to make the workplace better for people, most work still gets done through negative reinforcement. You can test this statement by reviewing the disciplinary procedures in your company's policy manual. If your company is like most others, the policy for discipline is elaborate, multiphased, and the result of many years of effort. Now compare it to the company's positive reinforcement policy. Do you have one? Is it written? Did the human resources department toil for months to develop it? If your company is like most of the ones I've visited, no effort has been made to produce a thoughtful, systematic positive reinforcement policy. Why is there such a wide discrepancy between what we believe and what we do?

BEING POSITIVE VERSUS POSITIVE REINFORCEMENT

Most people don't think there is a discrepancy between being positive and positive reinforcement because they consider themselves positive people. When conservative politicians say they want to take able-bodied people off welfare, they think that is positive because it will be good for the poor to get a job and become self-sufficient. When liberal politicians want to continue giving money to those who are less fortunate economically, they think that is positive because it will be good for the poor to get a helping hand. As you will discover, although both are well intentioned, neither solution is a good example of effective positive reinforcement.

I believe that most of society's problems result from the misapplication of positive reinforcement. Behaviors that are detrimental to a well-functioning society receive unintended positive reinforcement through poorly conceived laws and regulations and from the ill-informed people who administer them. This occurs not only at the general level of society but also at home, at work, and at play. Parents often inadvertently reinforce the selfish, lazy, and rebellious behavior of their children. Employees reinforce complaining and off-task behavior on the part of peers. People reinforce behaviors of friends that are detrimental to a lasting relationship. It is not uncommon for one spouse inadvertently to reinforce the quarreling of the other to the point where they no longer want to live together.

Practically no one would do these things intentionally. They happen inadvertently. Much of this could be avoided if people understood precisely how reinforcement works. However, most people have a very superficial understanding of the concept. When the process of positive reinforcement is presented as just common sense or something that you can do in a minute a day, you can expect that it will be greatly misused.

After more than 30 years of experience helping people use positive reinforcement to solve problems, I have found that when people make errors in delivering positive reinforcement, the errors usually fall into one of four categories: (1) the perception error, (2) the contingency error, (3) the delay error, and (4) the frequency error. This chapter will address the perception error.

THE PERCEPTION ERROR

Anytime you hear someone say, "Everybody likes…." you can be sure that she or he has made the perception error. There isn't anything that everyone likes. I hear managers say things like "Everybody wants more responsibility." That is not true because many people try all their lives to avoid responsibility. Consultants have told managers that employees want to make more decisions about their work. Believe it or not, some people want a job where they don't have to think and are just told what to do. Dr. Jonas Salk said, "The reward for work well done is the opportunity to do more." While this may have been true for him, there are a great many people for whom more work is punishing, not reinforcing.

There is nothing that everyone wants and likes and no single thing you can do that will please everyone. To use reinforcement effectively, you must know what reinforces a person's behavior. The perception error occurs when you perceive that something will reinforce a person's behavior when in fact it won't.

NOBODY DOESN'T LIKE SARA LEE

As the commercial goes, "Nobody doesn't like Sara Lee." While I will not dispute that assertion, I will say that it is about the only thing that nobody doesn't like. I have worked for years teaching managers that there are very few things that everybody likes. There is no "one size fits all," no one thing to do that will be reinforcing to everyone.

For instance, you may not be surprised to learn that not everybody likes public recognition. For example, surveys indicate that most people at work do not like to be singled out in public for a work accomplishment. Some do, but most don't. Nothing from money to pats on the back is reinforcing to all people in all circumstances. You probably can think of circumstances in which a pat on the back would be punishing or when offering money to someone would be insulting.

I have known managers and supervisors who were looking for "quick and dirty" reinforcers. By that I mean something that they could buy by the gross, such as key chains or pocketknives, to pass out whenever a person did something good. They often were disappointed in the results because the items they chose were reinforcing to so few.

KNOW THE REINFORCERS FOR THE PERSON YOU ARE TRYING TO INFLUENCE

To be effective with positive reinforcement you first and foremost must know the reinforcers for the particular person you are trying to influence. The perception error occurs when we treat people as we think they ought to be rather than as they really are. Parents often make this mistake because they know what their children "ought to like." They buy them clothes they ought to wear, take them to places they ought to see, and buy them CDs they ought to like.

The perception error also occurs when we assume that our reinforcers are shared by everyone. Because we like Greek food and the theater, we assume that our out-of-town guests will like those same things. Actually, what they really want may be barbecue and tickets to a football game.

The perception error frequently occurs when we assume that because a person is in a particular socioeconomic class, has a certain level of education, or is in a particular kind of job, he or she likes the same things most people in that group like. For instance, to assume that a truck driver doesn't like opera is a mistake; to assume that a Harvard graduate doesn't like to watch wrestling on TV also might be a mistake. Positive reinforcement is a very personal matter. Reinforcers cannot be applied to groups with the expectation that they will work for everyone.

Aren't there some things everyone likes? No, but there are some that come close. Attention is one of the first things that come to mind. Attention seems to be a powerful reinforcer for the vast majority of people. The variety of things people will do to get it, I am convinced, are endless. But while attention may seem to be a universal reinforcer, it is important to remember that throughout history there have been a few hermits.

GETTING TO KNOW YOU

The most important thing you can know about the other people in your life is their reinforcers. Most of the time we are so preoccupied with what we want or what we are not getting that we have little time or energy left for finding out what others want. Healthy, productive relationships, whether at home or at work, come about when two people know what the other one wants and needs and look for opportunities to satisfy that person.

When I was in clinical practice, couples who were having problems in their relationships rarely knew what the other person was about. It was surprising how few reinforcers they could name for their spouses.

If you take the time to learn another person's reinforcers, that person probably will call you "friend." Any time you make an effort to get to know what a person wants, needs, and values, you will gain that person's trust, respect, and loyalty.

HOW CAN YOU KNOW WHAT OTHERS WANT?

ASK

It is more difficult to find out another's person's reinforcers than it would first appear. How many times have you received a gift that you didn't like, need, or want? This occurs in every family among people who supposedly know each other well. The most obvious way to find out what someone wants is to ask. However, there are problems with that because in a large number of cases people don't know what they want. In my classes I ask people to make a list of their reinforcers. The average number that they list is about seven. In reality, everybody has hundreds, if not thousands.

Another problem with asking is that people often tell you things they think you want them to say rather than tell you what they really want. They may tell you things that are socially acceptable or politically correct because they are overly sensitive to possible censure. Many times people are unaware of what reinforces their behavior; the things they do that produce reinforcers are so much a matter of second nature that they do them automatically and have never thought about them in terms of the reinforcement process.

While it is acceptable to "ask," that obviously has limitations and should not be the only method used to determine what is reinforcing for another person. If you have a good relationship with a person, asking can be a quick, effective way to identify a reinforcer.

OBSERVE

Many times, however, it may not be appropriate to ask or you may not have the opportunity to do so. In these situations the method for identifying another person's reinforcers is to observe what that person does. How people spend their discretionary time and money is a great indicator of what reinforces them. Keep in mind, though, that people often spend time and money doing things they have to do, and so it is important to differentiate discretionary from mandatory behavior. Discretionary behavior shows more clearly than anything else what someone really values.

Remember that the real test is not how people say they spend their time or money but how they actually spend it. I have known people who say they value charity but give very little time or money to charitable causes. We've all known people who say their families come first, but when you look at their behavior, that is hard to believe because they spend very little discretionary time with them; other things always have a higher priority. You would not have to be around me for long before you realized that golf is an activity that produces a lot of reinforcers for me at this time in my life. I talk about it, read about it, buy all the latest equipment, and practice and play at every opportunity. Since that is easy to observe in my behavior, I naturally get a lot of reinforcers that are golf-related. Although the philosophical side of the actor Sylvester Stallone is not well known, he made an insightful statement when he said, "You are how you spend your time." Or as Gerald Rooney said, "Show me what you do and I'll show you what you believe in."

A key observational technique for identifying reinforcers is to see what someone does when she or he has a choice. If a person reads every chance she gets, you know that reading produces more reinforcers than do the other activities available at those times. If a person makes personal phone calls rather than work, you know that talking on the phone to friends is a reinforcer for him.

If you put a bowl of ice cream and a plate of cooked spinach in front of a 3-year-old child and ask him to choose, it is not difficult to predict what he will do. It would not be difficult to predict what would happen if you told a child that if she picked up her toys, you would give her some spinach. However, we cannot assume that every child will choose the ice cream, because occasionally one will choose spinach.

Not only do people vary in what they find reinforcing, what they find reinforcing changes over time. However, the fact that people change constantly is a problem only if we don't take the time to observe what changes are taking place. It's important to remember that we must treat people as evolving, unique individuals.

EXPERIMENT

The third method for identifying reinforcers is to experiment with a possible reinforcer and watch how a person reacts to it. If one potential reinforcer doesn't work, try another one. *Remember that positive reinforcement is defined by what the other person does, not by what you do.* If the behavior you are trying to reinforce increases or repeats, positive reinforcement most likely has taken place. If the desired behavior does not increase, it's time to try another potential reinforcer. It's worth the effort because once you are successful, you will have the power of the positive reinforcement process available to you.

You might be surprised at how effective experimenting can be. In my experience, most people are reinforced by another person's attempt to reinforce something they've done or recognize something they've achieved even though the particular verbalization or item was not desirable at that moment.

YOUR OWN LIST

I encourage people to make a list of their own reinforcers. It is an informative exercise. The initial list is usually quite short, as I mentioned earlier. Review it frequently and add to it. You will see later in the book how you can use this not only to increase your personal efficiency and effectiveness but also to increase the enjoyment and satisfaction you get out of life. In our company, everyone has a list, called a *reinforcer survey*, that is kept in a book in the front foyer. If anyone wants to do something to show appreciation for some effort or accomplishment of a fellow employee, he or she can refer to the survey to get some ideas about what is reinforcing to that person. Below is a partial list of my current survey.

Aubrey's Reinforcer Survey (A partial list)

Time with my wife and daughters

Anything related to golf

Watching sports on TV

Reese's Peanut Buttercup Blizzard

Pralines and cream ice cream

Reading scientific books and articles

Fixing things

Watching TV news programs

Going to movies

Archaeology

A cheese Whopper (hold the pickles and onions)

A baby's grip

Hearing about someone's success with R+

Pancakes at the Original House of Pancakes

Listening to classical music

Time at the beach

Time in the mountains

A joke (telling one)

> ## Aubrey's Reinforcer Survey (*cont.*)
>
> A joke (listening to one)
>
> Anything funny
>
> Old sayings
>
> Learning something
>
> A fire in the fireplace
>
> Surfing the Internet
>
> *The Far Side* cartoons
>
> Logo golf balls from clients
>
> Dessert (almost any kind)

CAN YOU ALWAYS FIND SOMETHING?

While it is true that some people's reinforcers are illegal, immoral, unethical, or socially unacceptable, that doesn't mean those people are unreachable. Everybody has so many reinforcers that even these people have reinforcers that are acceptable and can be used to strengthen desirable behavior.

Assuming that you have perceived one or more reinforcers, the next important considerations for making them effective are what and when to reinforce. That is covered in the next chapter.

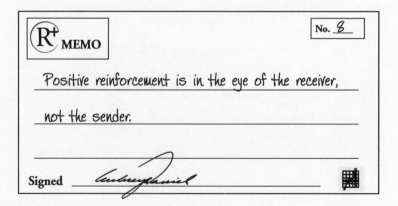

R⁺ MEMO   No. _8_

Positive reinforcement is in the eye of the receiver, not the sender.

Signed _____

9 CONTINGENCY
Behavior Followed by Reinforcement

If you give people something for nothing, you
make them good for nothing.

—A. DANIELS

In a *Good Housekeeping* article many years ago Henry Kissinger told a story about his former boss, President Richard Nixon. Kissinger was in the Oval Office in a meeting with the President, when a puppy, a recent gift, started chewing on a very expensive rug. The President told the puppy to quit. The puppy quit for a minute and returned to chewing the rug. The President shooed him away only to have him return yet again. Finally, in desperation, as the puppy was chewing the rug, the President opened the bottom drawer of his desk, pulled out a dog biscuit, and called the puppy away from the rug. At that point Kissinger said to the President, "Mr. President, you have just taught the dog to chew the rug."

Henry Kissinger understood a very important fact about behavior: *Reinforcers reinforce what is happening at the moment they are given.* It works that way with animals, and it works that way with humans. Most people understand that it works that way with animals, but because humans are able to reason and talk, nature lures us into thinking that reinforcers reinforce what people are told they are for. The fact is that like it or not, reinforcers strengthen the behavior that gets reinforcement whether you intend it or not. Quite a few problems in business and at home can be traced to this simple fact, and we can solve a lot of our interpersonal problems when we understand this truth about reinforcement. Let's look at a recent example of the contingency error at work.

In an effort to stem poor morale in the newsroom, the management of the *Washington Star* decided to give the news staff free coffee. They were dismayed to discover that the staff complained about the quality of the coffee. A behavior analysis would show that the consequence (free coffee) was given when the behavior (complaining) was occurring. If the free coffee was desirable, those with knowledge about the effects of reinforcement would predict that the staff would complain more, and they did. Management didn't necessarily do the wrong thing; its timing was off. If it had given the free coffee only after morale had begun to improve even a small amount, it would have obtained a much better result.

As a psychologist, I have had many couples tell me that the closest they got physically and emotionally was after a fight. Show me a couple for whom that is true, and I'll show you a relationship that will not last or one where the couple will drift farther and farther apart.

THE POWER OF IMMEDIACY

To verify the power of immediacy, we have to look no farther than our own homes to see how easy it is to get in trouble with our families in this way. Parents who give in to a child's temper tantrum do not want to believe that they are increasing the rate and/or intensity of the tantrums. However, their response (giving in to the child's demands) inadvertently reinforces the tantrums, something they would never intentionally do. It is not so much that the parents do the wrong thing as it is that they do things at the wrong time.

As has been pointed out, the best time to reinforce a desired behavior is when it is happening, yet for some people this seems like the least likely time to do so. When parents see children playing cooperatively, they are often reluctant to interrupt because they are afraid the children might start quarreling again. Supervisors don't want to interrupt employees while they are doing a good job because they are afraid the employees might stop working. *The fact is that when you reinforce while a person is doing what you want, the desired behavior will be strengthened.* If you reinforce after the behavior has stopped, you run into the possibility that behavior other than what you want may be occurring when you finally do attempt to reinforce. For example, if you want to thank someone for helping you with a task and as you walk up he starts complaining about a coworker, this is not a good time to thank him. Choose another time to say thanks. Pay special attention to what is happening when you are delivering a positive reinforcer.

Bobby Jones, the legendary golfer, recognized the problems that can be created when positive reinforcement is inadvertently linked to the wrong behavior. In his book *Golf Is My Game*, he reflected on playing in The National Championship at the age of 14 against the defending champion, Bob Gardner. Jones had a comfortable lead, but Gardner broke his spirit with scrambling shots on three consecutive holes and went on to win the match. Jones recalls:

After all these years I remember exactly how I felt as I walked onto the ninth tee, and I remember exactly what I did. I felt that I had been badly treated by luck. I had been denied something that was rightly mine. I wanted to go off and pout and have someone sympathize with me, and I acted just like the kid I was…. It is the keen, poignant, and accurate recollection of this episode which has caused me so often to be thankful that it happened just as it did. If I had won those three holes, or even two of them, I probably should have won the match…. Yet if I had won, what would have happened next? Not giving myself any the worst of it, I think I was a fairly normal kid of fourteen. But how many of us today can look back at ourselves at that age and be completely proud of the picture? I must admit that I had already become a bit cocky because of my golfing success in play against grown men. Had I won that championship, I should have been Amateur Champion.... I shudder to think what those years might have done to me, not so much to my golf, but in a vastly more important respect, to me as a human being.[1]

In my opinion, this example probably shows as clearly as anything why Bobby Jones was as successful as he was in all aspects of his life. It shows me that he understood that you must *earn* success and that if you are not aware of what the environment is reinforcing, success can ruin you. I doubt that a "cocky" Bobby Jones would have had the worldwide admiration he enjoyed during his lifetime.

THE CONTINGENCY ERROR: REINFORCING ONE THING AND EXPECTING ANOTHER

I heard a radio advertisement in which a hospital was advertising that it was so confident of the quality of its service that if a patient had a meal that was not hot, the patient would get five dollars off the bill. If the meal was late, the patient would get five dollars off the bill. If the medicine was late, the patient would get five dollars off the bill. There were about five ways patients could get a rebate.

Is this a good idea? Obviously, someone thought it was. I'm sure the hospital executives thought that the service was so good that the money that would be refunded would be minimal and the offer would be a good selling point in a competitive market. However, when we do a behavior analysis, we see that the behavior that got reinforced was complaining about the hospital's service. The more the patients complained, the more money they got off the bill. Patients were probably watching the staff like hawks and timing events as if they were in the Olympics. I'm sure there were arguments about whether a particular occasion met the criteria for the money. What the hospital was doing, whether it realized it or not, was paying patients to complain about the service. I think you'll agree that that doesn't sound like a smart thing to do. It illustrates one of the golden rules of positive reinforcement: *Be careful what you reinforce, because you're sure to get more of it.*

To understand behavioral contingencies, ask yourself, "What does a person have to do to get the reinforcer or reward?" You must remember that the *stated* contingency and the *real* contingency are often different. You are told that "hard work pays off," and then you learn that the goof-off who has seniority gets the promotion, raise, or other reward that you worked hard to get even though his level of effort and results did not equal yours.

Many companies are disappointed when they increase fringe benefits and discover that performance does not improve. If they understood behavioral contingency, they wouldn't be surprised because in order to get full fringe benefits in the average company, all that's necessary is for an employee to do only enough to stay on the payroll. Fringe benefits are the price employers pay to get good employees and possibly keep them longer. They don't improve performance.

I was listening to the evening news, and Tom Brokaw said, "After the commercial we have a story that will show you just how crazy our society has become." Naturally, that piqued my interest enough to watch. The story was about a disc jockey at a Fort Worth, Texas, radio station who in an effort to help the local library told his listeners that he had hidden money in some books in the library.

In the first hour something like 800 people came to the library to find the money. The TV cameras panned the library to show the viewers the aftermath. The floor was literally covered in books. The conclusion by Brokaw was that "people have gone crazy."

If anybody was crazy in this situation, it was the disc jockey. People responded predictably given the way the consequences were arranged. The behavior that paid off under this contingency was not to go to the library to look for and read or check out books and then possibly find some money. What paid off was to run to the bookshelves and pull the books, any books, from the shelves and shake them as hard and fast as possible to see if any money might fall out. Certainly, it would not pay to read anything!

A BEHAVIORAL CONTRACT

If you understand the concept of behavioral contingency, you can avoid most of these errors. The word *contingency* in this context refers to the relationship between a behavior and a reinforcer. In other words, "What do you actually have to do to get reinforced?" To determine the real contingency, you often have to examine what people who get reinforced actually did.

A behavioral contingency is basically a behavioral contract. It often takes the form, stated or implied, that "when you do A, you get or can do B." When explained in these terms, contingency raises the specter of bribery in many people's minds. It is of course not bribery as there is nothing illegal, unethical, or immoral about stating a desired behavior and a consequence. When done in the context of this book, it produces feelings of confidence and pride and is associated with efficiency and effectiveness.

Behavioral contingencies operate in all aspects of life. Everyone would agree that there is nothing wrong with saying, "If you sell this product, I will pay you a commission." There is also nothing wrong with saying, "If you clean up your room, I will give you a cookie," or "When you complete your homework, you can watch TV." Problems associated with contingencies like these are not the fault of the contingency but of the management of them. If the salesperson is given a commission when the paperwork has not been done, you will have problems getting paperwork done in the future. If the room is not cleaned to your satisfaction and you give the cookie, you will have rewarded poor cleaning habits.

By the way, the prize in the bottom of a cereal box is great example of a good contingency that is universally mismanaged. The unstated contingency is: When all the cereal is eaten, you can have the toy. Children learn very quickly that what you do is open the box upside down and get the toy or pour the cereal out when your parents aren't looking, get the toy, and then put the cereal back in the box.

The premier of the former Soviet Union, Nikita Khrushchev, understood behavioral contingency. He said in a speech before the Supreme Soviet, "People who show the best example in their work must receive greater material benefit." The communist system had great difficulty with this concept, and this is in large measure why it was bound to fail.

During a recent trip to China I came face to face with the major implications of a change in contingency. Several years ago the Chinese government set down production quotas as usual for the millions of farmers in that country but then made one change: *They told the farmers that they could sell the surplus and keep the money.* Not only has production increased, farms are producing goods and services not usually associated with farms. I even visited a farm where they were producing high-quality fireproof steel doors as a sideline and making excellent profits.

Benjamin Franklin as Behavior Manager

We had for our chaplain a zealous Presbyterian minister, Mr. Beatty, who complained to me that the men did not generally attend his prayers and exhortations. When they enlisted, they were promised, besides pay and provisions, a gill of rum a day, which was punctually serv'd out to them, half in the morning, and the other half in the evening; and I observ'd they were punctual in attending to receive it; upon which I said to Mr. Beatty, "It is, perhaps, below the dignity of your profession to act as steward of the rum, but if you were to deal it out and only just after prayers, you would have them all about you." He liked the thought, undertook the office, and, with the help of a few hands to measure out the liquor, executed it to satisfaction, and never were prayers more generally and more punctually attended; so that I thought this method preferable to the punishment inflicted by some military laws for non-attendance on divine service.[2]

In the final analysis, a behavioral contingency is about earning. The best reinforcers are *earned*, not given. The best way to ruin children for life is to give them everything they ask for and require nothing in return. A friend of mine says that a child's first lesson in socialism is a weekly allowance. The allowance usually is given independently of the behavior or performance of the child. While the parents may scold the child for poor behavior during the week, they often give the child the money at the end of the week and threaten to take it away if the bad behavior continues. When behavior gets too bad, the parents take the allowance away. This always seems arbitrary from the child's perspective because the child got it when he or she misbehaved in the past.

Because of the power of positive reinforcement, it should always be given in a thoughtful way. At times when you want to surprise someone with reinforcement, you should be aware of the behavior that is occurring when you give it. Once my daughter asked for a tape-cassette player. I told her that I would think about how she could earn it. I thought about it over a couple of days and didn't come up with anything. Then I thought, If I were to just give it to her, what would I reinforce? She does well in school. She has never given us any problems. She is good at home. So one night I surprised her with it as she was studying for a test. She earned it by exemplary behavior at home and at school, and she received it when she was behaving in a way that contributed to those results.

It is of serious concern when a parent can't differentiate between loving a child and loving the child's behavior. Some parents who see their children very little because of divorce or job demands think that loving a child means that they must accept all that the child does whether they like it or not. This is a mistake on the part of the parents and hurts the child. These parents are afraid that if they don't accept everything their children do and give them everything they want, their children won't love them. The truth is that if they do this, it is almost certain that their children won't love them. It is not that you don't love children, but sometimes they are more lovable than they are at other times. Ask yourself this question, "If I reinforce my child for this behavior will it help him grow up to be a more effective, happy adult?"

Among the worst advice you could ever give or get is to always be positive. As Benjamin Franklin said, "Praise-all and blame-all are two blockheads." Nothing denies our individuality or our uniqueness so much as the concept that what you give to one you must give to all. This practice has hurt governments (as in communism), unions, teams, and families. It is a serious problem when a business or government gets so large that it can't treat its employees or citizens on the basis of their performance. As Vince Lombardi is reputed to have said, "Nothing is more unequal than the equal treatment of unequals." My own version of that is: If you give people something for nothing, you make them good for nothing.

CONTINGENCY MANAGEMENT AS SELF-HELP

What self-management boils down to is the arrangement of behavior and reinforcers to produce good and effective habits. Grandma understood this when she told you, "When you eat your vegetables, you can have some ice cream." When you apply this to your own behavior, it is called self-management. Those who are good at self-management are said to have self-discipline.

The beginning of self-discipline is to identify your reinforcers and make a behavior contract with yourself: "When I do A, then and only then will I get or do B." As was mentioned in Chapter 8, making a complete list of your reinforcers is very helpful in changing your behavior. It allows you to make extensive use of contingency management. For example, I might say, "When I finish this chapter, I will play golf," or "When I exercise, I can eat dessert." The more reinforcers I identify, the more opportunities I will have to improve my self-discipline.

THE PREMACK PRINCIPLE

Dr. David Premack, a behavioral psychologist, made an important discovery about behavior that has come to be called the Premack Principle.[3] This principle states that *a high-probability behavior can serve as a reinforcer for a low-probability behavior.* In more practical terms it means that if you watch what people do when they have a choice, their choice identifies a reinforcer for them in that situation. If you consistently choose to watch TV rather than read a book, the opportunity to watch TV can be used as a reinforcer for increased reading. If you typically choose to do one activity in your job and neglect another, you can use the one you like as a reinforcer for the one you'd rather not do.

The Premack Principle is an ideal way to do contingency management because with it we are able to identify many opportunities for self-reinforcement throughout the day. Remember that when we choose to do one thing over another, we have identified a reinforcer in that situation. For example, as I am typing, I notice that I would like a glass of water. Premack would advise me to set a small goal, say, finishing this paragraph, and then get the water. In that small way I will reinforce working on this book. Repeating this strategy will make me more productive and increase my satisfaction with my work habits. (Excuse me while I get some water.)

The Premack Principle also provides us with the most effective time-management system known. Make a list of the things you have to do. Rank them from the thing you most like to do to the thing that you least like to do and then *start at the bottom.* If you start at the bottom, a curious thing happens. When you complete the last item on the list, the next one is more desirable. The farther you go up the list, the more reinforcing the tasks become.

If you are like most people, you will start at the top, but look what happens then. When you complete the first task, the next one is less desirable. The farther you go, the more punishing the tasks become. Is it any wonder that people who start at the bottom get two to three times more done than do those who start at the top?

My first deliberate application of the Premack Principle to my own behavior occurred when I was writing my doctoral dissertation, a most traumatic time in my life. I had some problems with subjects dropping out of the study, and the original statistical tool I planned to use was not appropriate. I spent weeks looking for alternative evaluative statistics, and when I found them, I agonized over how to write them up. I spent days in the library without writing one sentence.

My chairman suggested using the Premack Principle. If I wanted to drink a cup of coffee or get up and stretch, I would have to finish a sentence or a paragraph. If I had to go to the bathroom, I would do the same thing. To go to lunch, I had to finish the page I was working on. To go home I would have to finish a section. By using this method, I estimate that I was 10 times more effective than I had been up to that point.

Years ago when I was in clinical practice, a friend asked me to see his father, who he said was having bouts of depression. His father, a man in his late fifties, was a salesman of residential central air-conditioning and heating units. Sometimes he would go for several weeks with no sales. Then he might have several sales in one week.

He had a long streak with no sales this time and as a result was either going in late to work or missing days because of depression. When he was particularly depressed, he usually told his wife that he needed to get away and suggested that they spend the weekend in a place they owned in the mountains. His wife said he loved the mountain place but she didn't because he was usually irritable and depressed the whole time. He dreaded coming back to Atlanta and usually was unable to face the sales meeting on Monday, primarily because he had no sales to report.

After I had heard about his problems, I told him that I wanted him to set a daily goal for calls, on-site visits, and proposals, which I would review the following week. If he made a sale, he was to call me immediately. As it turned out, he made a sale on Thursday of the following week. When he called and told me, I said, "I want you to leave for the mountains this afternoon." Like many salespeople he resisted the idea. He said he thought he had finally gotten his old spirit back and could see several other sales on the horizon. He thought that it would be better if he stayed and worked on getting some of those sales closed. I insisted that he go and even called his wife to make sure that they went.

He had a great time in the mountains. He was excited about coming back and was even excited about going to the sales meeting.

By using the Premack Principle in this situation we were able to rearrange his environment to reinforce behavior that was consistent with excitement, enthusiasm, and enjoyment of his job and life. When we started working on his problem, he thought there was something wrong with him. He left understanding that the contingencies of reinforcement in his environment were wrong. I am happy to say that I have stayed acquainted with him for many years since and he has had no recurrence of the depression and is now happily retired. (While you turn to the next chapter, I'm going to get a cup of coffee.)

(R⁺) MEMO   No. 9

Be careful what you reinforce because you are sure to get more of it.

Signed _____

---

10 TIMING IS EVERYTHING
Understanding Reinforcement, Recognition, and Reward

Slight not what's near through aiming at what's far.

—EURIPIDES (484–406 BC)

REINFORCEMENT VERSUS REWARDS AND RECOGNITION

Because the distinctions between reinforcement, recognition, and rewards have not been clearly or consistently explained in the popular literature or understood in their applications, rewards and recognition are almost universally misused in all areas of life. Almost none of the organizations our company works with feel they get their money's worth from their reward and recognition systems. The very popular "employee of the month" program, one of the most common forms of recognition in business and government, is thankfully on the wane because it usually upsets more people than it reinforces. Unfortunately, the number of compensation and incentive plans used by business and government that have been scrapped after a very short, ineffective, but expensive life continues to grow.

This confusion also exists at home and at school. Parents try rewards for a while and then stop when they become frustrated because the changes in behavior or the results they expected, such as better grades, neater rooms, and chores completed without being told, don't occur. Teachers and educators have gone from rewarding the top academic performers to giving everybody awards. Many teachers have found that both procedures cause problems and have quit using them altogether. About once every few months someone on TV gives the parents of young children advice about whether to use rewards. Anyone who takes those recommendations seriously will be totally confused, because there is almost no consistency among them.

Because of such confusion, Alfie Kohn's book *Punished by Rewards*[1] hit a responsive chord in a lot of people. His basic message is that rewards are bad with a capital B and their use should be stopped. Can it be that the concept of giving rewards for work, the most basic concept in our economic and political system, is wrong? Some people certainly think so. A lot of emotion accompanies the discussion of whether rewards are good or necessary.

I believe that the emotion comes from the fact that as even the detractors would admit, rewards do change behavior. Rewards cause murder, war, prostitution, and many other ills of society. They also cause kindness, cooperation, and extraordinary acts of generosity and altruism.

REWARD, RECOGNITION, AND THE DELAY ERROR

In this chapter I want to clear up what I consider to be widespread confusion about rewards, recognition, and reinforcers. Much of the confusion results from a failure to understand the delay error. To understand the problem, it is necessary to define the terms, *reward* and *recognition*.

Rewards usually consist of something that has monetary value. Gifts, bonuses, trips, time off from work, merchandise, and of course cash are just a few of the things that are thought of as rewards. Rewards usually are related to results, not behavior. In business, the delivery of rewards is almost always delayed because they are planned and carried out by individuals representing the organization, not by the immediate supervisor. They are delayed at home because parents are usually waiting for a result to occur rather than focusing on the behaviors that contribute to the result. Because of these characteristics, rewards have surprisingly little impact on individual behavior.

Recognition is usually social in nature and involves giving something that has value only to the performer. A note of congratulation from someone you like or admire may have high value to you but no one else. Other common forms of recognition include plaques or trophies with the person's name on it. Recognition, like rewards, is almost always delayed. If recognition is well thought out and delivered correctly, it can have an impact on behavior.

By their very definitions, you can see that rewards and recognition are not bad. Gifts and merchandise are not bad things. A trophy or a note of congratulation on an accomplishment is certainly not a bad thing. It is not the forms of reward and recognition that cause problems; it is the way they are used. I have been around long enough to know that anything can be done poorly, and the delivery of rewards and recognition probably provides the best example. How do people get into trouble with them?

A REWARD MAY NOT BE A REINFORCER

One way people get in trouble is by rewarding and recognizing a result or performance in ways that are not reinforcing. You may recall from earlier chapters that reinforcement is in the eye of the receiver. Reinforcement occurs during or immediately after the behavior it reinforces.

When we attempt to deliver some type of social reinforcement for a desired behavior, we know we are successful by the increase or repetition of that behavior. Rewards and recognition don't have the advantage of occurring close to the behavior they intend to reinforce, and so success or failure is often difficult to evaluate. They also have several other disadvantages. First, they suffer from the "one size fits all" problem mentioned in Chapter 8. The limited variety of available rewards and forms of recognition may not be desirable to the recipients. An employee of a manufacturer of small airplanes told me that after 25 years of service employees got a ride in one of the company's planes. He laughed as he told me this. He said, "Not only would no one work 25 years to get to do this, but many people are afraid to fly in them." The reward was not reinforcing to many people because of its size in proportion to the work involved and because of its very nature. A gold-engraved pocket watch or even a small cash award may not be desired or valued because of the circumstances under which it is presented.

To be effective, rewards, like reinforcers, must be personal. As much care should go into determining what form a reward should take as is done with a positive reinforcer. We all have clothes we have received as presents that have never been worn, gadgets we've been given that don't get taken out of the box, and knickknacks that quickly find their way to a box in the attic or basement. The best rewards are things a person wants to buy or do but doesn't feel he or she can afford.

Cash is not the best reward because unless it is given in large amounts, it is soon gone with little to show for it. The advice to "buy something for yourself" is rarely followed, and the money is spent on a bill or repair. While small amounts of money can be very effective with young children, they are not effective with adults. For adults, a $20 cash award often is laughed at as insignificant for some work-related performance. However, even when the rewards and recognition are desirable (are positive reinforcers), they are still problematic because of the inherent delay between the time when the behavior occurs and the time when rewards and recognition are delivered. Therefore, most of the problems with rewards and recognition are due to timing.

REWARD AND RECOGNITION OFTEN REINFORCE THE WRONG BEHAVIOR

Not infrequently, the behaviors that merited a reward or recognition are no longer occurring when the reward is delivered. This means that since positive reinforcers reinforce the behavior that is occurring when they are received, rewards and recognition actually may increase the wrong behavior.

When you understand that rewards are by definition delayed rein-forcers, it is easy to see how they reinforce the behaviors that are occur-ring when you get them, not what you might have done to earn them. If is not uncommon in business for a reward and/or recognition to occur so late or be so unpredictable that the recipients may be angry or burned out by the time they get it. Guess what the result is? Do you think receiving the recognition or reward under these circumstances will cause an immediate change in a person's behavior? Don't count on it. *Remember that you may not get more of what you reward, but you will always get more of what you reinforce.*

PROPERLY DELIVERED RECOGNITION AND REWARDS INCREASE REINFORCEMENT

If a person receives positive reinforcement day to day, a reward just adds value to a reinforcing relationship with the presenting person and organization. If you have a positive relationship with someone, the problems associated with rewards are minimized. Even if the reward fails to reinforce the right behaviors, at least the person will like you more because of the pairing of the reward or recognition with you.

Rewards never get a good response if day-to-day interactions are punishing or are based on negative reinforcement. Parents and employ-ers who pressure, goad, or threaten day to day and then offer a reward for an accomplishment are disappointed in both the emotional response and the subsequent behavior of the recipients. It is not uncommon under such conditions for the rewarded performance to stop after the receipt of the reward or recognition or for the person to verbalize negative feelings toward the giver.

A friend told me about someone in her office who was complain-ing bitterly to her about how incompetent she thought management was. Just then her boss interrupted to tell her friend that she had been named "employee of the quarter." After the manager left, the woman said to my friend, "Well, I guess that proves my point. If they think I'm the best employee here, they really are incompetent!"

While one might think that getting the award would change her opinion, it strengthened her present behavior: complaining about management. To avoid this mistake, ask yourself, "If I give a reward at this time, what behavior will I reinforce?" The answer to that question, as you know by now, is whatever the recipient is doing when he or she gets it.

Many parents have gotten themselves in trouble after a child has earned a reward, because by the time they get around to delivering it, the child is angry, irritable, or depressed. To give it at this time is to reinforce angry, irritable, or depressive behavior. The parent and the child would be better served by waiting until more appropriate behavior is occurring to give the reward. In my experience, when I gave rewards under such circumstances, my children didn't enjoy them much. Therefore, you should wait until they are behaving in a more positive way. In this way, the reward will be more meaningful and effective. Never give a reward, even when it has been earned, when the present behavior is something you would not like to see more often.

BRIBERY VERSUS REWARDS

A question I must have been asked a thousand times, particularly as it relates to children, is, "But isn't that bribery?" Many parents think that saying to a child, "If you do your homework, I will give you some ice cream," is bribery. My response is that it is no more bribery than the statement "If you do this job, I will pay you a salary." Both are merely statements of behavioral contingency. The typical parental response is, "But aren't there some things that children should do just because they are members of the family?" While I certainly agree that there are some things everyone in the family should do, the question usually remains, "Do they do them?" If they don't do things to help around the house, it is almost certainly because they have not been positively reinforced for helping. They don't necessarily need to be rewarded for every little thing they do, but they definitely need to be positively reinforced for their good behavior.

Michael Popkin, the author of "Active Parenting," says, "But if you reward kids for something they ought to be doing anyway, they will expect it. They won't answer the doorbell unless they know they will get paid for it."[2]

This is poor advice from at least two perspectives. First, kids, like adults, do what they do because of the consequences they receive. If they are not doing something you think they should be doing, the first thing you should do is examine the consequences you have established for doing and not doing the behavior in question. It might be that the child can sit in front of the TV, bark orders, and get everything he wants while Mom pleads with him to answer the doorbell or clean up his room. By contrast, if you arrange conditions so that when the child does the things that he *ought* to do, he gets more of what he wants, there will be no problem.

The second part of this issue is that if a child does not respond to the doorbell until she is promised a reward, you know that you are reinforcing the wrong behavior. You may discover that you are inadvertently reinforcing statements such as "Whadda ya gonna give me?" rather than a class of behaviors called "being helpful."

DELAY IS DEADLY: THE DELAY ERROR

Because of the delay between a behavior and a reward many things can happen, and most of them are bad. Since you often don't know what people did to get a reward, you may find that you have reinforced the wrong behavior or even the wrong person. Tom Sawyer got Huckleberry Finn to paint a fence for him. While Huck was rewarded for doing good work, Tom was rewarded for finding someone else to do his work. It is not a problem to pay children for good grades if in fact they are studying and learning the material. While I am not advocating this, I don't find it as reprehensible as do some so-called behavioral experts. It should be obvious at this point that the best time to reinforce is when you catch someone in the act of doing something appropriate. If you do that, you will have much more confidence that you will get more of what you want.

Because of the problems associated with the inevitable delay between behavior and recognition and rewards, there needs to be some way to bridge the gap between previous behavior and current behavior. An effective way to do that is to give the person an opportunity to relive the accomplishment. We have a saying in our company, "Reinforce behavior; celebrate results." If you do not personally see the behavior, the only way you can reinforce it is to celebrate it. From a behavioral perspective, a celebration is not about food and drink but is an occasion to ask questions of the person such as "How did you do that?" This gives people an opportunity to tell you how smart they were, how difficult the task was, and how hard they worked. Such conversations are positively reinforcing to almost everyone.

The best recognition and rewards are ones that anchor a memory of an accomplishment. This often rules out money because money is quickly spent and the memory of it soon fades. In a recent TV interview the winners of an international ice skating pairs competition were asked, if they had to choose between the money they made by winning the tournament and the trophy they received for that competition, which would they take? Without hesitation, they both said, "The trophy." We all have things that we cherish that have no economic value to anyone but us and that we consider priceless. Many times they are things we have kept since childhood. In times of flood, fire, and other disasters that threaten people's houses, the things people save are first the pictures and then other things that have a story to tell. Trophies, trinkets, and all sorts of awards can be priceless, but only if they anchor memories of accomplishments or positive events.

If you look at the behaviors that consistently occur in your presence, you will have a good picture of what you are reinforcing. If you don't like them, you probably are using reinforcement, recognition, or rewards in an ineffective way. By attending to the details of this chapter and the previous ones on positive reinforcement, you will find that recognition and rewards can be used in a way that brings joy to you and those around you.

RELATIONSHIPS: THE KEY TO SOCIAL REINFORCEMENT

The only way to maximize the effect of reinforcement, recognition, and rewards is to establish positive relationships with those around you. You do this by establishing yourself as a reinforcing person to them. To do that, you have to look at your ratio of positive interactions to punishing interactions. If most of your comments are complimentary, if you keep the promises you make, and if you demonstrate interest in others' problems and try to help, you most likely will be viewed as a positive element in their lives. For a parent this doesn't mean that you have to be a "pal" to your child. You don't have to give into every whim or indulge every request. What it does mean is that you have to pay a lot more attention to the good things children do. Talk to them about the little successes they have every day instead of having meaningful conversations only when there is a problem or when they "screw up." In this way, any attempts you make to reinforce, recognize, or reward will be received in the spirit in which they are given. At work, if you approach coworkers only when you need their help or when something they did caused you a problem, they will become defensive as soon as they see you. With that kind of relationship, any attempts you make to reinforce, recognize, or reward will be viewed with suspicion and any value the reward or recognition might have will be diminished. In the final analysis, positive reinforcement is not about things; it's about relationships.

R^+ MEMO

No. 10

It is hard to celebrate when you have been beat up on the way to the party.

Signed

11 TOO MUCH OF A GOOD THING?

Give me enough ribbon and I will conquer the world.

—NAPOLEON

U
nfortunately, Napoleon ran out of ribbon somewhere in Russia,
but it's clear that he understood the power of recurrent positive
reinforcement. I frequently hear the comment, "I reinforced her,
but she didn't change." My response is always, "One reinforcer will not
change your life." This is the frequency error. The fact is that one reinforcer will not change behavior permanently or significantly. Most often
it will only create a small change that may be hardly noticeable and
probably won't last.

Remember that when we are interested in influencing behavior, we
are usually interested in changing undesirable habits. A single reinforcer does not create habits, which typically involve many behaviors.
As Mark Twain said, "Habit is habit, and not to be flung out of the
window by any man, but coaxed downstairs a step at a time."[1] If you
are to be successful in changing your own habits or helping others
change theirs, it will require many, many reinforcers.

This is actually good news for those who worry about delivering
positive reinforcement. Newcomers to the process frequently ask,
"What if I make a mistake and reinforce the wrong behavior?" The fact
that it requires many reinforcers to create a habit should provide some

comfort. *One mistake doesn't make or break a habit.* Reinforcing the wrong behavior is a problem only if one reinforces it repeatedly.

LESS POSITIVE REINFORCEMENT IS NOT ALWAYS BETTER

Some people have the mistaken idea that less reinforcement is better than more. Samuel Johnson said in *The Rambler,* "Praise like gold and diamonds owes its value to its scarcity." Benjamin Franklin apparently agreed with him when he wrote, "Praise little, dispraise less." However when it came to his own behavior, he had a different opinion. Franklin said, "[D]id not my Writings produce me some solid Pudding, the great Deficiency of Praise would have quite discouraged me." While a lot of people would agree with Sam and Ben, all the research points to the fact that in practically all situations people reinforce too little, not too much.

One finding revealed by the behavioral researchers Kent Johnson and Joe Layng is that when children receive hundreds of reinforcers an hour, they make progress in learning at unheard of rates—four to six times the normal rate.[2] The hardest classes in school and the hardest jobs in the workplace are not the ones where you have to do a lot but the ones where you have to do a lot with little or no reinforcement. Think about this in terms of sports. If you want to know why sports is a more desirable activity than work or school, look at the difference in the frequency of reinforcement in each area. Every play in sports gets reinforcement from teammates and fans. It is also interesting that in sports, players are usually reinforced for the effort whether it is successful or not. "Good try," we shout. "Atta way to catch." "Good swing." I do not think it is a coincidence that sports are the preferred leisure activity for millions of people. If I am playing golf when I am 100 years old, I do not believe I will ever get tired of hearing people say, "Good shot!" I cannot imagine that I will ever turn and say to them, "Good shot, good shot, good shot. That's all I ever hear. I'm sick of it. Don't you think I know it's a good shot?"

An old fellow once told me, "When I got married, I told my wife, 'I love you, and if I change my mind, I'll tell you.'" Think he's still married? Unfortunately, this is how most people think of reinforcement. "People know I appreciate what they do" is a comment I've heard many times. A man in one of my classes told me that on his first day at work his boss called him to his office, and as the boss was laying down the ground rules, he said, "Now I'm not one of these people who go around patting people on the back and all of that, so I want you to know today that I appreciate everything that you will ever do for this company." I have known people who have carried letters of praise from the boss in their pocketbooks for years. When they pulled them out, the letters were fragile and worn, looking more like a Civil War document than a note from the boss they had received 5 or 10 years earlier. The fact that these complimentary letters were scarce may have made them valuable from a collector's perspective but not from the standpoint of creating, increasing, or maintaining good work habits.

Think of reinforcement as the fuel or energy needed to keep behavior going. When behavior runs out of fuel, it stops. A reinforcer does not provide perpetual motion as some people seem to think. People often ask, "How long do I need to reinforce?" My response is, "How long do you want the behavior to continue." Any behavior that is not reinforced, will eventually stop. You can't reinforce it once or for a short period of time and then forget it. It is good to remember the child's poem: "Tell me you love me. You told me once but I forgot."

HOW MUCH IS ENOUGH?

Just how much reinforcement is enough is an empirical question. If a behavior is increasing or is occurring at a desirable rate, it is probably getting enough reinforcement. If it begins to fall off, it probably isn't. If you remember not to take good behavior for granted and continue to reinforce intermittently, you probably will keep the behavior going indefinitely. A good rule to follow is to *reinforce more than you think you should.* If you think you are reinforcing too much, you're probably doing about the right amount.

One way to know if someone is getting enough reinforcement is to observe how focused the person is on the task at hand. Reinforcement commands attention. In other words, one's attention doesn't wander under high rates of reinforcement. Watch children playing a computer game or another fast-paced game. They are often oblivious to what is going on around them. People who are highly distractible are usually people who are in an environment with too little reinforcement.

The behaviorist B. F. Skinner estimated that in order to learn basic arithmetic, the average child needs over 50,000 reinforcers.[3] Figuring that on average a student receives 700 total hours of math instruction from grades 1 to 4, this comes out to more than 70 reinforcers per hour. Of course, when you hear these numbers, you realize that a teacher cannot be the sole source of reinforcement for academic work; this also gives you an understanding of how inadequate the general notion of reinforcement frequency is.

The obvious question is, "If a teacher is unable to personally deliver these high rates of reinforcement, how can it be done?" The answer is that it is the teacher's job to create a structure and arrange a learning environment where the right behaviors are reinforced in the right way, at the right time, and at the right frequency. This is what teaching is all about. By now you should realize that the prospect of getting an "A" many months down the line is rarely enough to keep a student motivated throughout a semester.

A teacher has at least three ways to make reinforcement occur many times an hour. One way is to arrange the learning environment so that high rates of reinforcement are possible. Frequent practice sessions are a requirement for frequent reinforcement. Academic material on computers is not always designed with reinforcement rates in mind, but those materials produce higher rates than traditional materials do and can potentially rival computer games for reinforcement frequency. Another source is the teacher, but teachers are not typically taught to reinforce at high rates. However, several studies show that when they do, discipline problems disappear and achievement soars.

The teacher can get some help in reinforcement from the student's family by sending assignments home, and students paired as learning partners are in a position to deliver dozens of reinforcers to each other during practice sessions. Teachers who learn to use their students as coaches enjoy extraordinary success. Of course, in addition to teachers, family, and peer coaches, the fourth source is self-reinforcement by the students themselves.

EXTRINSIC AND INTRINSIC REINFORCEMENT

The ability to reinforce yourself (intrinsic reinforcement) is directly related to the amount of external reinforcement you have received throughout your life. Concepts such as self-confidence and self-esteem are not things we are born with, but things we learn. The good feelings that accompany accomplishments are learned. As such, they can be traced to early experiences of learning to walk, talk, and do things for ourselves. As positive reinforcement is paired with the many accomplishments of childhood, most people develop the ability to "reinforce oneself" at the completion of a task, even a long or complicated one. However, the thought that "I'm pleased with what I've done" or the good feeling associated with accomplishment can come only from previous similar experiences in which external validation was received. In other words, *you can't be proud of yourself till somebody's been proud of you.*

HOW MUCH IS ENOUGH?

In a survey of the literature on "learned industriousness," Dr. Robert Eisenberger, a psychologist at the University of Delaware, concluded that reinforcement history, specifically a history of being positively reinforced for high effort (hard work), produces positive effects on people's self-control, moral development, persistence in the face of failure, and general work ethic.[4] He quotes Dr. J. B. Watson, one of the first psychologists to focus on studying behavior rather than the mind, as was common in his day. Watson said that "the formation of early work habits in youth, of working longer hours than others, of practicing more intensively than others, is probably the most reasonable explanation we have today not only for success in any line, but even for genius."[5] This was written in 1930. Research since that time has consistently validated his conclusion.

In *The Achieving Society*, Dr. David McClelland, a Harvard psychologist, states that

> *both the mothers and fathers of the boys with high* n *Achievement (the Achievement Motive) set higher standards of excellence than did the mothers and fathers of boys with low* n *Achievement. They tended to expect their sons to build higher towers, to copy block patterns of greater difficulty, and to stand further away from the peg in the ring-toss game. This finding clearly confirms all the evidence already cited that one of the ways in which a child can develop low* n *Achievement is through having careless or indulgent parents who do not expect great things of him.*
>
> *The second measure I derived from the voluminous record of the things the parents said to their boys during the experimental session. Rosen and D'Andrade labeled it "warmth," because it involved a "combination of positive tension and positive evaluational acts, indicating generally pleasant, happy, anxiety-relieving, laughing-joking behavior ... and provides a measure of the amount of positive affect the parents put out while the boy is working. The finding is especially interesting because it confirms a difference in the reaction to success reported by mothers of sons with high and low* n *Achievement in Winterbottom's study. There, too, the mothers of the "highs" reported that when a son succeeded at something they more often "kissed or hugged" him, presumably showing, as here, their greater emotional involvement in his success.[6]*

Although McClelland does not use the term *positive reinforcement,* it is easy to see that that is what he discovered. The mothers and fathers of high-achieving children clearly delivered a higher frequency of positive reinforcement when interacting with their children than did the parents of low-achieving children.

It would be great if everybody grew up under conditions where reinforcement was frequent. However, many children grow up under conditions of negative reinforcement and punishment and thus do not internalize the ability to feel good about much that they have done. Hart and Risley provide an insight into this in *Meaningful Differences in the Everyday Experiences of Young American Children.*[7] The authors and their colleagues practically lived in the homes of parents with children under age 4 and recorded millions of interactions between the parents and their children.

They looked at three socioeconomic groups: professional, working class, and welfare. They discovered that there were significant differences in the frequency of verbal interactions between these groups, ranging from an average of approximately 45 million in the professional group to approximately 13 million in the welfare group. However, in my opinion, the relative number of interactions is not as important as the quality of those interactions. I am referring here primarily to the ratio of positive to negative interactions during this period.

In the professional group there was a ratio of approximately 6:1 positives to negatives per waking hour. The working-class group had a ratio of about 2:1, but the welfare group had a ratio of roughly 1:2. In other words, the children of welfare parents were twice as likely to have a negative interaction with the parents as a positive one. What this amounts to over the first 4 years is that in the professional group, a child will receive over a half million more positive interactions than negative ones, and the children of the working-class group will receive about 100,000 more positives than negatives. However, in the welfare group the children will receive almost 150,000 more negatives than positives.

Is it any wonder that children on welfare grow up to be cynical about life and negative about themselves and their future? It also is not surprising that the children of professionals grow up feeling that they can accomplish their dreams. An important thing to understand about these numbers is that since they are averages, they don't describe individual families. I am sure that there are professional families that are more negative than the welfare average; I am also sure that there are families on welfare that are as positive as are professional families. I grew up in a working-class family, and I am sure that the ratio in our family was greater than 2:1. However, on the average, these data show some very important differences and point to a very practical intervention with families. It is very easy to increase the number of positive verbal interactions with children. This is something that parents can track. Increases in positive reinforcement rates by the parents could be rewarded as Risley did with teachers in some early studies in classrooms.

Risley and his associates found that the ratio of positives to negatives in classrooms was low.[8] They set up a system where teachers were paid to find things in the students' performance about which they could say something positive. This intervention resulted in increased achievement and improved discipline in the classrooms. Even if we could not have much impact on the parents, the school could focus on increasing the rate of positive reinforcement and have an ameliorating effect on the low rates at home.

Remember, you don't give people "self-esteem." They have to earn it. But you can be alert to increased opportunities to help them earn it.

CHANGING TIMES: THE "NINTENDO GENERATION" HAS ARRIVED

I have often been asked by supervisors and managers as to why positive reinforcement is so necessary today whereas it was not important when they were hired. The answer lies in a change that has gone almost unnoticed in business and education: *Reinforcement rates in all aspects of life are increasing almost exponentially.* Because the rates of positive reinforcement 50 years ago were very low in comparison to today, it took considerably less to keep focused at work, at school, and at home. Today computer technology has produced products that can deliver reinforcement at rates never dreamed of just a few years ago. Things that took hours and days to do in the past now take seconds.

Increasing rates of positive reinforcement are radically changing the pace of life. The effects can be seen in individuals ranging from the TV channel surfer to the Internet surfer. Many people think that attention spans are getting shorter. They are not. It is just that people today, especially young people, have so many opportunities to engage in activities that produce high rates of R+ that they move quickly from those which don't to those which do. Young people have no problem spending long periods of time playing computer games or surfing the Internet because of the high rates of R+ they receive.

VIDEO AND COMPUTER GAMES

Computer games provide one of the clearest examples of an activity with a high reinforcement rate. If you understand positive reinforcement in this case as pushing a button and having something happen on the screen that you like or want, you can understand the fascination large numbers of children have with these games. The average child playing a computer game will probably get in the range of 70 to 100 reinforcers per minute. This is more than children get from practically any other part of their environment. It explains why game playing is preferred to schoolwork or jobs around the house. Television ads aimed at young people move from one scene to another at the rate of about once a second. Look at a channel such as MTV and note how many scene changes occur per minute. The rapidity of movement frustrates me but is attractive to young people. This is the world they grow up in. Sound bites are what people want. Many "in-depth" interviews on TV today take less than 2 minutes.

The reality of these rapid rates of reinforcement has not been lost on businesses that sell consumer products. Since the rate of changing behavior is associated with the rate of reinforcement, attracting customers depends on how much reinforcement a product delivers. Therefore, without even knowing it in a scientific sense, businesses have been on a fast track to see how much reinforcement they can put into their products or services. This usually is done under the name of features such as "ease of use," "multiple applications," and "new and improved." But in the scientific analysis, it is obvious they are really increasing the rate of reinforcement for using their products or services.

The frequency of reinforcement required to maintain the interest of many young people is way beyond the frequency that is generally available in the typical workplace. There are few jobs that produce the 70 to 100 reinforcers per minute that are available with video and computer games. Dramatic changes in the level of reinforcement will have to be made to accommodate the new generation of employees.

This new generation of workers, the "Nintendo Generation," began arriving at work in the early 1990s. They are creating problems that business doesn't know how to handle, primarily because business doesn't understand reinforcement as anything other than a smile, a wave, and a pat on the back. New employees accustomed to rates of reinforcement not even dreamed of in my day find themselves bored in a very short time. It is not unusual for a member of the Nintendo Generation to come to the boss after a week on the job and ask, "What's next?" The boss will, of course, respond, "Whadda you mean what's next?" "Well, I did that job for a week, and I want to know what I'm going to do next." The boss will respond, of course, "I want you to continue doing what you did last week. That's your job." "No," the employee says. "I've done that. I want to do something new." The motto of the Nintendo Generation is "Been there, done that."

Managers who do not understand reinforcement think that the solution is to have people rotate jobs, be involved in all decisions, and have increased responsibility. This is a mistake in many instances because such practices may increase costs, decrease quality, and decrease responsiveness to the customer. What young people are saying when they want to do something different is that they are not getting enough reinforcement in the current job to maintain their interest or attention.

Think about it for a moment. People who play computer games do not play a different game every time. Some people have been playing the same computer game for years. New games are being developed and marketed all the time (the new game promises to be more reinforcing than the last one), but the behavior is exactly the same. The person sits, sometimes for hours, pushing buttons. The repetition is not a problem as long as there is adequate reinforcement for doing it.

BEHAVIOR GOES WHERE REINFORCEMENT FLOWS

Given that the general level of reinforcement in our environment is accelerating, we are faced with the fact that if we want to influence behavior successfully, we are going to have to provide accelerated levels of reinforcement. This is the case because we are competing with a barrage of reinforcement from many sources, and all things being equal, behavior moves to the most reinforcing part of the environment.

It seems to me that the practice in business of having employees compete for reinforcement among themselves is a model that has outlived its usefulness. This competition results in too many behaviors chasing too few reinforcers. In a situation where a manager recognizes the best performer, only one is rewarded and many are punished. Things such as "employee of the month," "salesperson of the year, and "student of the month" limit reinforcement rather than increase it. These practices come from the myth that seeing another person get an award will inspire the others to improve their performance to get it next. The reality is that for every employee who is inspired by seeing someone else get an award, 20 probably will experience disappointment, discouragement, or anger. Awards and other recognition for "best, first, and most improved" are almost always divisive.

Because most sports are created to provide high rates of reinforcement for the participants, competition is not as detrimental as it is in situations where the rates are low. In business, in education, and in the family, competition is usually detrimental and should be used only to have fun in situations where "bragging rights" are the only reward. Since we want everyone to win in those settings, reinforcement needs to be available to all who earn it.

In the future, positive reinforcement will be built into jobs that are performed on the computer, just as it is in computer games today. Employees will have immediate feedback on performance as it relates to past performance and progress toward goals and standards. Tangible and social reinforcers will be triggered by things such as improvement, quality levels attained, and individual best-ever performance.

By now you realize that the use of positive reinforcement is not a love 'em and leave 'em approach. Whether you are working to change your behavior or the behavior of others, frequent reinforcement is the key to success. Can you do it too much? Not if you do it right!

THE FOUR ERRORS REVISITED

Doing it right means avoiding the four common errors. You do that by making sure that (1) the reinforcement is meaningful to the recipient, (2) the reinforcement is earned, (3) it is immediate and (4) it is frequent enough to sustain and even increase the desired behavior. If these errors are avoided and these guidelines are followed, you will be surprised at the power of positive reinforcement to make changes in your life and in the lives of those around you.

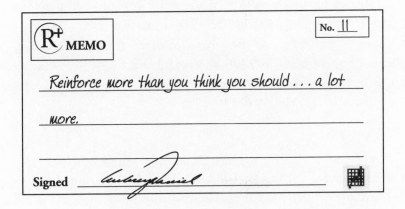

R⁺ MEMO

No. 11

Reinforce more than you think you should . . . a lot more.

Signed

12 PMF
Pinpoint–Measure–Feedback

> I often say that when you can measure what you are
> speaking about, and express it in numbers, you know
> something about it; but when you cannot measure
> it, when you cannot express it in numbers, your
> knowledge is of a meager and unsatisfactory kind.
>
> —LORD KELVIN
> *Popular Lectures and Addresses*

Every serious athlete has PMF. No, it's not a medical condition; it refers to the fact that athletes know how to *p*inpoint precisely what they need to do, have some way to *m*easure what is being done, and have some way to translate the measure into *f*eedback. When you add positive reinforcement to these three factors, you have a powerful formula for problem solving and helping people do their best in sports, at work, and in their personal lives. All four—pinpointing, measuring, feedback, and positive reinforcement—are necessary to influence human behavior consistently and effectively. If you omit one, you reduce your chances of solving a problem or enhancing behavior.

PINPOINTING

In all my years of helping people solve problems at home and at work, the most difficult part has always been determining the specific behav-

---

ior that would improve the situation. People are much more likely to know what they *don't want* others to do than what they *want* them to do. But even when they describe what they don't want, they talk about it in nonbehavioral and very general ways. Parents say: "Don't do that." "Leave that alone." "Be quiet." Friends complain: "She has a bad attitude." "He has a big ego." "She is afraid of her shadow." Coworkers say: "He is the most hostile person I know." "She's as lazy as it gets." "He is totally uncooperative." "She is really up-tight."

It is helpful to identify what we don't want or don't like only to the extent that it leads us to identify the behavior we do find desirable. For example, if coworkers are concerned that one of their peers is becoming "too bossy," it would be helpful to that person if they would advise him to "ask for others' opinions" and "compliment others more often" rather than telling him he is "too bossy." Telling someone that she is "too negative" would not be as helpful as telling her to "smile more" or "say more positive things" or "talk about things you like." You must be specific when identifying the behavior you find desirable. It is the difference between telling a friend to "act confident" and suggesting that she "try to maintain eye contact when talking to someone."

In one of our performance management classes we asked the students to choose a self-improvement project they could implement immediately so that they could see the effects of reinforcement on their own behavior. Many would choose weight reduction. Later, they would complain that on breaks we had sweet rolls, candy, and other "calorie- and fat-laden" snacks. They did not think it was fair for us to do this since they were trying to lose weight.

I pointed out that this was the fairest thing to do because it was only in the presence of "forbidden food" that the behavior they wanted to change could occur. The desirable pinpointed behavior is to choose nutritious alternatives over fattening ones. Going to a "fat farm" is an easy way to lose weight because you can't make the wrong choice, but you don't get to practice the behavior that will solve your problem in the long term. This is one of the reasons weight loss is very often only temporary. An old saying applies here: "It is easy to be prudent when nothing tempts you to stray."

The first step in solving a problem with yourself or someone else is to answer the questions, "Precisely what do I need to do? Precisely what do they need to do? What specific behavior is required?" Solving almost all problems requires an active behavior, yet people consistently talk about solutions in terms of stopping a negative behavior. Dr. Ogden R. Lindsley, a pioneer in behavior analysis, came up with the "dead man's test" to help people determine whether they were in fact focusing on an active behavior.[1] It may be more politically correct to think of this as the "pet rock" test. The principle is this: *If a pet rock can do it perfectly, it won't solve your problem.* Can a pet rock make no errors, have no accidents, have no complaints, be at its desk, not be negative, have no fights, have no arguments, and not misbehave?

Casey Stengel, the longtime manager of the New York Yankees, knew how to turn a phrase. He said, "If the fans don't come out to the ballpark, you can't stop them." It is not difficult to stop people from doing something that they are not doing. What is more difficult is to find ways to motivate fans to come see a losing team; this was Casey's problem with the early Mets. The point is that to solve a behavioral problem, people must do something active, not inactive. Pet rocks can't be active. As I have mentioned several times, *stopping a negative behavior does not guarantee that an appropriate one will take its place.* If you know what you want, you will be more likely to reinforce it when you see it. Sometimes focusing on what you want eliminates a step in problem solving. If you increase a desirable behavior, the problem behavior often disappears. For example, when attempting to stop an unsafe behavior, we recommend dramatically increasing the behavior that is safe. In this way you eliminate the unsafe behavior by crowding it out with safe behavior.

While general descriptions of problems communicate general patterns of behavior and are usually sufficient for day-to-day communication, they are not sufficient to solve a behavior or performance problem. *A precise description of the desired behavior is needed.* If you can observe it and describe it to another person and that person can observe it and then you both can count how often it occurs and come up with the same number, chances are that you have pinpointed the desired behavior well enough to begin to try to improve the situation.

Dr. Laura Schlessinger, the radio therapist, has an amazing skill at pinpointing behaviors that need to be changed and identifying who needs to change them. Listeners can understand what the problem behaviors are and what needs to be done to change them. While they may not agree with her analysis or choose to follow her advice, they have little doubt about what she is telling them to do.

Most relationship problems result from the inability to specify a problem behavior and the appropriate ones that should take its place. Remember, if you can't specify the problem behaviorally, you can't see appropriate behaviors when they happen. And if you don't know when they are happening, you can't reinforce them.

MEASUREMENT

Many times a problem is defined not by the behavior but by its frequency. For example, let's say you have worked with someone for 10 years and have never seen him cry at work. One morning you walk into this person's office and see him with his head in his hands, sobbing quietly. If you are like most people, you will ask what is the matter and if there is anything you can do. Let's say that another person has been working for the same period of time and has been known to tear up about something at least once a week. If you walked in on this person crying, you might try to back out of the office without being noticed.

The behavior is the same. The frequency is the problem. Someone who gets angry occasionally would not be considered to have a problem; someone who is angry every day would. This means that some way of tracking the frequency is not only helpful but often necessary.

If this sounds like measurement, it is. I've noticed that there is a lot of resistance to measuring behavior in some areas of our society and no resistance at all in others. For example, we don't reject measurement in sports; we demand it. Sports wouldn't be nearly as interesting without "stats." But in other aspects of life we resist measurement, calling it dehumanizing and superficial. Business provides the most common examples.

Having worked in business for many years, I have heard about every excuse you can name for why it is impossible to measure certain jobs. This is said primarily because in much of our business experience we have seen that measurement has been used to punish rather than reinforce. Numbers are used to determine who is at fault, who didn't make the quota, who to fire. In sports, measurement is used to determine which behavior to reinforce and who to reward. This makes a big difference in how people respond to measures. People rarely object to being called "the best," but determining the best assumes some ordering or measuring.

Psychiatry frustrated me because there were practically no reliable behavioral measures of progress. The diagnoses did not lend themselves to easy measurement. For example, Dr. Otto Fenichel, a prominent Freudian scholar, says that agoraphobia, or fear of open spaces, "is often a defense against exhibitionism or scoptophilia. Scoptophilia, the sexualization of the sensation of looking, is analogous to touch eroticism. Sensory stimuli which are normally initiators of excitement and executors of forepleasure may, if too strong or repressed, later resist subordination under the genital primacy."[2] Get it? Neither do I.

Explanations such as these never made sense to me. What does this description tell you to do if you have agoraphobia? Of course, all Freudian diagnoses are defined in a way that requires you to get help from a professional to understand them. They do not deal with behavior because behavior is assumed to only be a symptom of some deep-seated underlying problem that is manifested only indirectly through inappropriate or maladaptive behavior. Not surprisingly, some people love these kinds of diagnoses. They are mysterious and usually are related to sex in some way. They also are very reinforcing to anyone who does not want to be personally responsible for his or her behavior or the improvement of his or her situation.

I have always been too pragmatic to understand such complicated diagnoses. When I had a patient with a phobia, I would try, to the extent possible, to put that patient in the situation he or she feared and see what the patient did. If patients were afraid of elevators, I would put them in an elevator and see how many floors they could ride. Not surprisingly, at first most would not even get in the elevator even if the power was off. I would start slowly to change their behavior. If they had agoraphobia, I would take them to the front door of the clinic and see how far they would go down the sidewalk before they would have to come back.

By approaching the problems in this way, I was able to get a measure of the pretreatment baseline of the phobia, from which I was able to evaluate the success of the treatment. I developed measures with all my patients, and I never had one complain about it. Their expectation and experience was that the measurements were designed to help them with their problems. They all felt more in control of their progress and more confidant about their success. When measurement is done correctly, that is the outcome.

Although many people think that tackling problems with measures overly simplifies the situation, the truth is that measures clarify complex problems and make it possible to solve them effectively and efficiently. They allow you to quantify the actual extent of a problem and provide a framework for evaluating your solutions. This advantage of measurement is very valuable because in both business and personal life people tend to overreact and/or underreact to situations. One advantage of measurement is that is helps keep a problem in perspective.

Courtney Mills, one of our performance management consultants, was working with a senior manager of a large textile firm. The manager, Max, was responsible for 13 plants. He conducted cost meetings in the plants every month. The meetings were traumatic because Max was very punishing. When Max learned about positive reinforcement, he realized that he did not do much of it and knew that he needed to change. He asked Courtney to help him make the meetings more effective. Courtney said that he would count the number of positive and negative comments Max made during a meeting.

At the end of a 90-minute meeting Courtney had counted 54 negative comments and no positives. On seeing the data, Max responded, "I knew I was bad, but I had no idea I was that bad." I have heard this said many times when people see data on their behavior. I have often said, "If you don't have the data, you don't know what is happening. The data will surprise you every time." Keep in mind that data also can surprise you in a positive way. You may be making more progress with a project than you think. Without measurement, small improvements can go by unnoticed and projects that might have resulted in something worthwhile can wind up being abandoned because of a lack of positive reinforcement.

One of my colleagues told me after a 20-minute speech that I had used the phrase "you see" 32 times. I couldn't believe it. I protested, and as I was talking he said, "You said it again." I didn't even hear it. However, as he kept pointing it out to me, I began to hear myself saying it. Since I realized that it was distracting to my audiences, I asked him to track it in my speeches. Once I had a count, I could tell that I was improving as the numbers went down. I was excited about seeing how much I had improved after each speech.

At a clinic where we were consulting, the nurses complained that when patients had to wait to see the doctor, the nurses got all the negative consequences. We asked the nurses to keep the data on "patient waiting time." The data showed that patients waited an average of 55 minutes—not good. Upon seeing the data, every doctor said, echoing the manager from the textile firm, "I knew it was bad, but I didn't know it was that bad." The reinforcement strategy the nurses used was to help any doctor who reduced waiting time by doing some of that doctor's charting. By measuring the improvement, the doctors were able to see that within 2 weeks, they had reduced average patient waiting time to 20 minutes and were coming up with ideas almost every day about how to improve it even more.

If you look at the biographies of people who achieved extraordinary accomplishments, you find that they had some way to measure their behavior or performance. Many had diaries that they reviewed on a daily basis, and others had more formal systems. B. F. Skinner measured and graphed how long he spent writing every day, among other things. Benjamin Franklin developed a self-improvement project that was quite detailed and, according to his account of it, very successful.

It was about this time I conceiv'd the bold and arduous project of arriving at moral perfection. I wish'd to live without committing any fault at any time; I would conquer all that either natural inclination, custom, or company might lead me into. As I knew, or thought I knew what was right and wrong, I did not see why I might not always do the one and avoid the other. But I soon found I had undertaken a task of more difficulty than I had imagined. While my care was employ'd in guarding against one fault, I was often surprised by another; habit took the advantage of inattention; inclination was sometimes too strong for reason...

I included under thirteen names of virtues all that at that time occurr'd to me as necessary or desirable, and annexed to each a short precept, which fully express'd the extent I gave to its meaning.

These names of virtues, with their precepts, were:

1. Temperance.—Eat not to dullness; drink not to elevation.

2. Silence.—Speak not but what may benefit others or yourself; avoid trifling conversations.

3. Order.—Let all your things have their places; let each part of your business have its time.

4. Resolution.—Resolve to perform what you ought; perform without fail what you resolve.

5. Frugality.—Make no expense but to do good to others or yourself, *i.e.,* waste nothing.

6. Industry.—Lose no time; be always employ'd in something useful; cut off all unnecessary actions.

7. Sincerity.—Use no hurtful deceit; think innocently and justly, and, if you speak, speak accordingly.

8. Justice.—Wrong none by doing injuries, or omitting the benefits that are your duty.

9. Moderation.—Avoid extremes; forbear resenting injuries so much as you think they deserve.

10. Cleanliness.—Tolerate no uncleanliness in body, cloths, or habitation.

11. Tranquility.—Be not disturbed at trifles, or at accidents common or unavoidable.

12. Chastity.—Rarely use venery but for health or offspring, never to dullness, weakness, or the injury of your own or another's peace or reputation.

13. Humility.—Imitate Jesus and Socrates.

My intention being to acquire the *habitude* of all these virtues, I judg'd it would be well not to distract my attention by attempting the whole at once, but to fix it on one of them at a time; and, when I should be master of that, then to proceed to another, and so on....

I made a little book, in which I allotted a page for each of the virtues. I rul'd each page with red ink, so as to have seven columns, one for each day. I cross'd these columns with the first letter of one of the virtues, on which line, and in its proper column, I might mark, by a little bleak spot, every fault I found upon examination to have been committed respecting that virtue that day.

I determined to give a week's strict attention to each of the virtues successively. Thus, in the first week, my great guard was to avoid even the least offence against *Temperance,* leaving the other virtues to their ordinary chance, only marking every evening the faults of the day. Thus, if in the first week I could keep my first line, marked T, clear of spots, I suppos'd the habit of that virtue so much strengthen'd, and its opposite weaken'd, that I might venture extending my attention to include the next, and for the following week keep both lines clear of spots. Proceeding thus to the last, I could go thro' a course compleat in thirteen weeks, and four courses a year ... I hoped, the encouraging pleasure of seeing on my pages the progress I made in virtue, by clearing successively my lines of their spots, till in the end, by a number of courses, I should be happy in viewing a clean book, after a thirteen week's daily examination.

This my little book had for its motto these lines from Addison's *Cato:*

> *Here will I hold. If there's a power above us*
> *(And that there is, all nature cries aloud*
> *Thro' all her works), He must delight in virtue,*
> *And that which he delights in must be happy.*[3]

	Sun	M	T	W	T	F	S
Tem							
Sil	•	•		•		•	
Ord	•	•			•	•	•
Res		•				•	
Fru		•				•	
Ind			•				
Sinc							
Jus							
Mod							
Clea							
Tran							
Chas							
Hum							

Although I would recommend a chart that tracked positive instances of each virtue, Franklin's method seemed to solve the problem quite well. The fact that Franklin continued this project for several years is a testimony to its utility and effectiveness.

FEEDBACK

Feedback is necessary to all learning. You don't learn to walk, talk, read, write, or ride a bicycle without feedback. Feedback allows you to see what you are doing and make corrections in the desired direction. Feedback is simply information about performance that allows people to change or improve that performance. In many situations the immediate consequences provide correction or confirmation for the behavior. Our senses are constantly giving us sensory and kinetic information about our behavior in relation to the environment.

A child learning to walk gets frequent feedback from her body and surroundings that helps her learn to maintain her balance as she attempts to move forward. The oohs and aahs from the family also reinforce her first steps. In learning to ride a bicycle, off-balance sensory feedback provides information to counter a sensation of leaning to the left by making an opposite movement of leaning to the right. And so it goes in learning to drive a nail into a board with a hammer, steer a car, or correctly shape letters as one learns to write. These situations don't usually require formal feedback because the immediate consequences are inseparable from the feedback.

The most common use of the term *feedback* in social interaction is in the form of "let me give you some feedback." What that usually means is that someone wants to give you negative information about something that you have done or didn't do. This turns out to be punishing most of the time.

When I use the term *feedback* in this context, I mean graphic feedback. In our consulting practice we emphasize the many advantages of putting behavior and results measures on a graph. You can see progress easily, you can see progress over time, and you can see how change in behavior relates to achieving subgoals and final goals. Benjamin Franklin knew the value of a visual display of his progress.

The best job you will ever have is one where you know how you did at the end of every day. Most people will never have that kind of job, and their enjoyment will be reduced accordingly. I wish I had kept track of all the parents who saw "miraculous changes" in their children's behavior when they worked out a system of reinforcers and rewards and put up a daily graph of progress. It must be thousands by now.

There are countless examples of how PMF used in business applications created an increase in effective positive reinforcement and led to successful behavior change. Here are a couple of memorable ones.

The first example took place in the accounting department of a transportation company called Preston Trucking. The manager was showing me the many graphs they were using to track the department's progress on a number of improvement projects. It was obvious that a lot of positive reinforcement was occurring there not only because of the increases in performance but also from the smiles and comfortable interaction between supervisors and clerks. As we were talking, the manager showed me a note that had been left by a part-time employee. The note read, "Mr. Cook, can I please have a graph like Mary Jo? P.S. I did 41 invoices in 56 minutes. I timed myself." She had seen how much reinforcement other full-time employees were receiving by graphing their progress and didn't want to be left out.

A motel chain also had great success with measurement and feedback. As we all know, one of the problems with housekeeping is that you do it, someone messes it up, and then you have to do it again. This hotel chain was experiencing inconsistent cleaning practices among their housekeepers. Things changed dramatically when we developed a checklist to measure the cleanliness of the rooms and gave the housekeepers graphic feedback on their scores. The managers were convinced that measuring the housekeepers performance would "run them off." Of course, they thought this because they had used their previous measures to show the housekeepers what they were doing wrong. This system was used to show them what they were doing right, and they loved it. After they experienced the positive reinforcement that was paired with the graphic feedback, they almost always wanted to know immediately how they had done when they saw their rooms being scored.

Another advantage of graphing is that it provides a picture of a performance long after the performance has been completed. For example, a housekeeper could see that she had scores above 900 (1000 was perfect) for 3 months in a row. I have recommended this system to homemakers who have complained about "hating housekeeping" and to others who have had problems with family participation in keeping the house clean and neat. I suggested that they develop their own checklists and scoring systems so that each family member could see graphically how well he or she was doing. This allowed much more positive reinforcement because individual and family progress was visible for all to see.

This system is also effective for personal performance with sports. For instance, I could not get myself to jog until I posted a graph of my times and distances. I graphed them religiously for years and continued to jog for more than 25 years. I don't jog now as much as I used to. I'm sure one of the reasons is that I do not currently keep graphs. I do keep a graph of my weight and have done so for 24 years. Below is a graph showing the results from my recent high-protein diet.

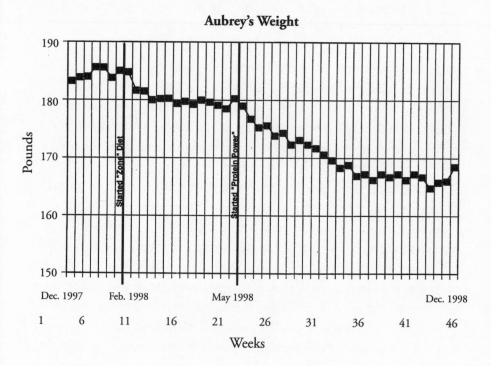

Aubrey's Weight

The combination of feedback and reinforcement forms a very powerful behavior change tool. Below is a typical example from the workplace.

The Percentage of On-Task Behaviors of Employees at a Pizza Store

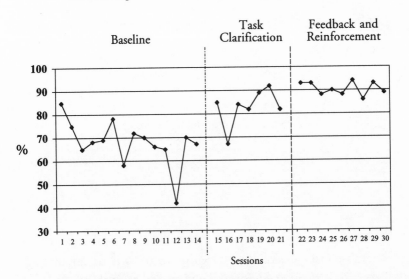

SOURCE: Jon S. Bailey, Ph.D., ed., Progress in Performance Management v 8: 85, 1999.

Keep in mind that pinpointing, measurement, and feedback work together to set up increased opportunities for reinforcement. They are necessary and very helpful for improving performance, but they are not sufficient. If positive reinforcement is not forthcoming, even the best PMF will have a limited impact on behavior.

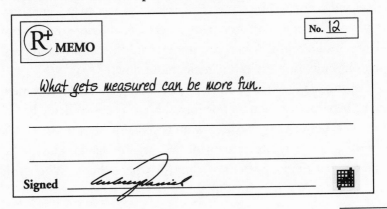

13 MAKE HASTE SLOWLY

Nature does not proceed by leaps.

—CAROLUS LINNAEUS
Philosophia Botanica

The most critical skill in changing your own or anyone else's behavior is *shaping*. Shaping is a technical term that is defined as "the positive reinforcement of successive approximations toward a goal." It is more commonly referred to as "one step at a time." This procedure capitalizes on the fact that change generally does not proceed by leaps and bounds but through a number of small changes that often go unnoticed by the casual observer. Interestingly, the smaller the change in behavior that you can observe and reinforce, the more effective you will be in changing behavior and the faster the change will occur. While reinforcing small changes may seem slow, it is actually the fastest way to change behavior because reinforcement increases momentum. When you understand this, you will understand Benjamin Franklin's advice to "make haste slowly."

Shaping requires that you start reinforcing small improvements in current behavior as soon as possible. This is quite difficult because if someone is performing way below an acceptable level, most people set an initial goal for reinforcement of the target behavior close to where the performer ought to be, not close to where she is. When you ask people to name the person who had the most influence on their careers, it is not unusual for them to name not a parent but a teacher, coach, relative, or friend. The reason for this is that many parents are lousy teachers for their children. They expect their children to learn more, faster, and better than the kids next door. The neighbor, uncle, aunt, or schoolteacher who had a significant influence on them accepted them *where they were* and provided reinforcement for the slightest interest, effort, and improvement.

Something I have noticed over the years is that expert parents frequently don't have children who follow in their footsteps professionally or in their hobbies or other interests. I think I know why: Expert parents as a rule are not the most adept at the shaping process. I know a parent who loved tennis but was not very skilled. In city league competition he was at the lowest skill level, but he loved the game. When his son was not much taller than the racket, Joe had him on the tennis court. Because the father was not an expert, he was unable to hit the ball to his son with any accuracy, and so he brought a basket full of tennis balls to the court and would toss them to his son to hit. When his son would tip the ball and it would go careening off the court, Joe would shout, "You hit it, Son. Good! Here, hit this one." His son would hit as many as the father would throw and then beg for more.

Contrast that with another father-son duo. This father is what would be called an A player; that is, he plays in the most skilled league. He brings his son to the court, stands on one end of the court, motions his son to stand on the other end of the court, and says, "Here, hit this one." The father hits a ball that clears the net by about an inch. The son swings mightily at the ball, sending it back across the net. The father yells, "How many times have I told you to get the head of that racket down and back? You're never going to learn to play this game if you are not ready. Now, if you are not going to do it right, you might as well not play it at all. Here, hit this one."

Which of these boys do you think is a tennis pro today? Of course, it is the first. *Experts usually see too many things that are done wrong to reinforce small things that are done well.* Perfectionists usually make bad teachers because they tend to reinforce only when something is done perfectly. They use common strategies that produce high failure rates in learning. They demand too much, too soon and fail to see and reinforce small improvements.

Have you ever had teachers who knew the subject so well that they couldn't teach it? What I say about those people is that "they forgot what it's like not to know." The first father still knows how it feels to get his racket on a hard serve and avoid getting aced. It is therefore easy for him to reinforce his son for just getting a racket on a ball that he throws to him. For the second father, hitting the ball back over the net is what is expected and therefore, in his eyes, requires no reinforcement. The second child ended up playing soccer. Guess what his father knew about soccer!

The real skill in teaching and coaching is knowing where to start. The most successful teachers are those who can break down subject matter and tasks into the smallest steps and then reinforce at every step along the way. Those who are skilled in this process of shaping are able to see a behavioral path to the desired target. In other words, the behavior you reinforce initially is not the behavior you reinforce in the final step. It is not unlike Michaelangelo seeing David in a rough chunk of marble. The finished product is clear in the creator's mind's eye, but the creator produces it one stroke at a time.

MOVING MOUNTAINS

Because the behavior psychologist and author Dr. Ted Ayllon is a pioneer in the use of behavioral technology in the family, he gets the toughest cases to solve. His success in solving them is legendary. His approach, however, is one that anyone who wants to change behavior can use. After listening to the problem presented to him and carefully defining the behavior to be changed, he usually says something on the order of, "Today, I want you to continue doing what you have been doing, but *make this one small change.*" Who can't continue doing what he or she is now doing and make only one small change? This is very easy advice to follow.

Dr. Ayllon knows that he must make change easy not only for the *changee* but for the *changer* as well. He would agree with the ancient Chinese proverb "He who would move mountains begins by carrying away small stones."

The story is told that Thomas Edison once described the process by which his company made the first commercially viable light bulb by saying, "I found 10,000 ways *not* to make a light bulb." I don't know how he actually managed day to day, but his approach of eliminating options that don't work seems like an ingenious way to positively reinforce the completion of tasks that are far removed from a final, desired outcome.

For example, suppose he assembled his experimenters, called "muckers," and said the following: "In the entire world there are probably 10,000 materials that we can try that might prove to be a satisfactory filament for a light bulb. Out of that 10,000 there are probably only about 10 that will work. Your job is to find the ones that don't work." With the problem conceptualized that way, when a mucker yelled out, "Tom, Tom! I tried oak, and it doesn't work," Edison could shout in return, "Hey, everybody. Bob tried oak, and it doesn't work. Mark it off your list. We're one step closer to a solution." This method provides a minimum of 10,000 opportunities for positive reinforcement along the way to a solution. Think how depressing it would be if the only reinforcement came from finding the final solution. (By the way, they actually did try oak!)

This method can work just as well today. For example, if sales professionals know that 1 out of 20 people called will buy, every time they get a no, they know they are closer to a sale. This will work in any situation where success has a low probability and persistence pays off.

THINK SMALL TO ACCOMPLISH BIG

Goals should be set so that the probability of reaching them is high. Failing to do this is a very common mistake people make in attempting to improve their performance or that of others. It is not wrong to have lofty ambitions, but if you don't have many opportunities for reinforcement along the way, you probably will fail.

I have seen many people who, in trying to change some aspect of their behavior, set themselves up for failure right from the start because their beginning goals are too ambitious. For most people a goal of losing 2 pounds a week is too ambitious. They may be able to do it for a couple of weeks, but doing it longer than that is usually too difficult.

It is better for them to set a goal of losing 1 pound a week and then cut it to a half pound after several weeks when weight loss becomes more difficult than it is to set it at 2 pounds and fail. Most people who try to stop smoking by going "cold turkey" fail. When I was in clinical practice, I helped many people stop by getting them to reduce the number of cigarettes they smoked per day by one each week.

The best advice you can get for setting goals is to set them *too low.* If you set them too low, the *probability of reaching them is high.* Success is usually reinforcing or as the saying goes, "Success breeds success." *You can never go wrong reinforcing improvement—no matter how small.* If you are oriented toward reinforcing any improvement, no matter how small, you will never run out of something to reinforce. The best teachers, coaches, supervisors, and parents are the ones who can see the smallest change in behavior or performance and positively reinforce it.

Many people think that when you talk about setting low goals, you are compromising standards and can't achieve excellence that way. In reality, it increases the chance that you will be able to reach and exceed the highest standards. Look at positive reinforcement as behavioral fuel. The more fuel you have, the longer you will be able to stay with a difficult task.

In the business world, it is difficult for many managers to understand that the fastest way to change an organization is by making thousands of very small changes. These managers fall into the trap of setting "stretch goals," one of the most misunderstood concepts in management today. Those who set stretch goals have succumbed to the commonsense notion that higher goals will get people to do more than they would if the goals had been set lower. But because stretch goals focus on results, not behaviors, this process typically reduces the opportunities for positive reinforcement, reducing the chances for ultimate success.

KNOWING WHERE TO START

As a consultant to a prevocational training center for mildly retarded students, I was asked to give some suggestions about how to handle a boy the psychiatrist had diagnosed as an "oppositional character." What that meant was that the boy would do the opposite of what one asked. If you asked him to sit down, he stood up. If you asked him to stand up, he would sit down. If you tried to trick him and ask him to do the opposite of what you wanted, he would figure that out and still not do what you wanted.

The center had a token economy in which the students could earn the opportunity to play games, watch TV, read, or do other activities. To earn the tokens, they had to make progress in some area of work or work habits. I suggested to the supervisor that when he went back to the work area, he should ask the boy to bring him his token card so that he could give him enough tokens to watch TV. He looked at me and said, "Wouldn't that be giving him tokens for nothing?" "No," I replied. "You would be reinforcing him for doing something you asked." On each subsequent request the supervisor was to ask a little more of him: "Bring me a pen and your card and I'll mark it so that you can watch TV." "Add up your points, bring me that pen, and I'll give you what you need to go to the game room." By the middle of the next week this "oppositional character" was participating like all the rest. By reinforcing small steps along the way, the supervisor was able to help the boy make significant changes in a short time.

For people who don't know how to shape, this scenario may seem too easy to be realistic, but I have seen hundreds of cases where seemingly intransigent behaviors have been changed in a relatively short time with this simple technique.

Another example of how shaping can influence behavior happened when ADI consultant Courtney Mills was teaching performance management to a group of textile supervisors. After the introductory lecture he asked if the class had any questions. No one did. Then he asked if they had any comments. A supervisor who had been sitting in the back of the room with his chair leaning against the wall, looking like he was smelling something bad the whole time that Courtney had been talking, said, "Bull!" At that time, Courtney was big on using silver dollars as reinforcers because people would keep them. He didn't miss a beat. He walked back to the supervisor, pulled out a silver dollar, slapped it down on the desk in front of him, and said, "I want to positively reinforce you for telling me what you think. I know exactly where you are coming from. I'm not so sure about the rest of these fellows, but me and you are going to get along great!" Rather than be offended by a crude remark, Courtney saw an opportunity to reinforce a behavior that could be shaped to something more productive. Of course, the supervisor turned out to be a star in using performance management (PM) in his job. While he was just as loud and opinionated, now he was pro-PM, not anti-PM.

Dr. Loren Acker of the University of Victoria in Canada developed a computer program to teach students how to shape behavior.[1] The object of the exercise was to move a figure called Sidney from one side of the computer screen to the other as fast as possible. While the students wanted to keep Sidney moving on a straight line (the shortest distance), if the reinforcers (keystrokes) were not timely and frequent, Sidney would deviate from the straight and narrow. With this simple exercise Dr. Acker learned two things about how people typically reinforce. The primary thing he learned was that people are stingy even with reinforcement that doesn't cost them anything. The students constantly required too much movement before they delivered reinforcement. In other words, they set their goals too high and provided too little reinforcement along the way, and the result was that Sidney moved up or down or even backward. That led to the second thing Dr. Acker learned. If at some point the students didn't reinforce *any* movement, no matter how much it deviated from the horizontal, the figure would stop. Of course when Sidney stopped, the exercise was over and so was the potential of influencing Sidney's behavior.

From this experiment Dr. Acker came to two conclusions with which I certainly agree:

1. Be generous with your reinforcement.
2. Realize that without behavior, no change is possible.

This means that on some occasions you may need to reinforce behavior far removed from your eventual goal. In other words, sometimes you may need to reinforce behavior that may be in opposition to your final goal in order to get any behavior to shape.

In any negotiations, for example, whether in the family, business, or international politics, the object should be to keep talking. When you keep talking, you have a chance to shape the eventual outcome. Unfortunately, in many difficult interpersonal situations at all levels of society, the parties, not understanding reinforcement, reinforce the wrong behavior and shape away from the ultimate goal. When you understand reinforcement, it is possible to convert some of the worst situations into the most stunning successes.

To understand the power of the Asian proverb "Many raindrops make an ocean," think what would happen in your family, company, or community if all the members made a small improvement in something they did every day. How long do you think it would take to make a significant difference in these groups? A week? A month? Certainly no longer than that. Do the math. This formula means that a family of four would make 4 improvements a day, 28 a week, 92 a month, and 1104 a year. Think of what it would mean for a company of 400 or a community of 40,000. We know the power of the atom, a particle too small to see. When many atoms are massed together, the result is awesome. The same is true for behavior. One small change may be limited, but when little is added to little, it can be family-changing, company-changing, life-changing, and even world-changing. As Benjamin Franklin said, "Human felicity is produced not so much by great pieces of good fortune that seldom happen, as by little advantages that occur every day."[2]

R⁺ MEMO   No. 13

People who reinforce the smallest improvements get the fastest change.

Signed _Aubrey Daniel_

---

14 DOS AND DON'TS OF DELIVERING POSITIVE REINFORCEMENT

The manner of giving is worth more than the gift.

—PIERRE CORNEILLE
LE MENTEUR

David Thompson says, "Indeed, from a profit point of view, what people say to each other and how they say it probably has more influence than any other kind of interaction in private industry. Verbal interactions can make or break a company."[1]

I certainly agree that what people say to others and what they don't say have more impact on what gets done than all the computers and machinery in business. Whether a computer runs at all or whether a machine is fixed in a timely manner usually depends more on the verbal interaction between people than the physical or intellectual skills of those involved. Dr. Murray Sidman says that everybody knows how to punish but relatively few people know how to positively reinforce.[2] The ability to use positive reinforcement effectively is a skill, and although some people acquire it naturally, most people have to learn it.

A story is told about Yogi Berra, the Yankee catcher and manager, who was attending a reception one summer afternoon given by New York's Mayor Wagner and his wife. As Yogi approached Mrs. Wagner in the receiving line, she looked at him dressed in a silk-flowered, short-sleeved, open-collared shirt and said, "Yogi, you look mighty cool today." Never at a loss for words but never knowing what form they might take, Yogi responded, "You don't look so hot yourself!" While Mrs. Wagner, undoubtedly knew what Yogi meant, in many cases people know only what they hear. Everyone has been in situations where someone took something the wrong way. Something that was intended to be a compliment may turn out to be a punisher. As my mother has said to me on several occasions, "Good intentions pave the road to hell."

For the purposes of this chapter, verbal interactions include not only what people say but also what they write or express by gestures and other body language. Frowns and smiles communicate a lot. A "thumbs-up" and an extended middle finger also communicate a lot. There are also times when saying nothing communicates effectively.

How can we make sure that we communicate what we intend? There are a few simple rules that will increase the probability that your positive reinforcement will match your intention.

RULE I: ESTABLISH YOURSELF AS A REINFORCER

If people don't like you or don't want to be around you, nothing you say will have the effect you want. If they like you, even when you make mistakes, they will assume you meant well. We assume that Mrs. Wagner was not offended by Yogi's remark and that she understood that it was an innocent mistake or an example of Yogi's unique way with words. Had she not liked him, however, she might have been offended and might not have thought it was an innocent mistake. She liked him because nobody could not like Yogi. He had a way with words that always brought a laugh or a smile. Therefore, he could probably say anything to anybody. He had established himself as a reinforcer to almost everybody by his past behavior.

The way you establish yourself as a reinforcer is to pair yourself with reinforcers. You do this by increasing the frequency of your attempts at reinforcement. Make a conscious effort to see the good things others do and comment on them, and you will be perceived in a more positive light. By doing this, you will find that people will want to be around you. They'll value your opinion because you value theirs.

When people like you, your reinforcing ability is enhanced. Dale Carnegie said, "Getting people to like you is only the other side of liking them."[3] Establishing good relationships can be as simple as treating people with kindness and using good manners. Finding things of interest in others is of course another way to be appealing to people and establish yourself as a reinforcer.

RULE 2: DON'T FAKE IT

It should go without saying that sincerity is the foundation of effective social reinforcement. A Hollywood mogul was quoted as saying, "Sincerity is everything, and if you can fake it, you've got it made." The problem is, you can't fake it for very long. As David Thompson says, "If a man's tie is ugly, it will do no good to compliment him on his choice of clothes. There are too many ways in which insincerity can be detected, including subtle changes in voice, facial expression, and body movements."[4] Charges of manipulation often result from suspected insincerity. Say only what you mean and only what you are comfortable with if you want your reinforcement to be successful.

RULE 3: DON'T USE FLOWERY LANGUAGE

Contrary to what most people think, social reinforcement doesn't require flowery speech with lots of adjectives and adverbs strung together, such as "the most beautiful, exciting, wonderful thing I have ever seen." As a matter of fact, this kind of speech is more often punishing than reinforcing. Few people like someone who gushes over something they have done. It is often more reinforcing to talk about things "getting better" or comment on a small improvement you've noticed.

Vary the words you use to tell people that they are appreciated and that their performance is valued. "Have a nice day!" has been said for so long that it no longer has special meaning. Pat phrases such as these lose their reinforcing value quickly, and their frequency causes them to appear false. Saying "Good job" to someone may be very reinforcing, but if that is all you ever say, its sincerity will quickly come into question.

Positive reinforcement doesn't depend on words. Many times if you take words at face value, you miss hidden meanings. Comments that at first seem punishing may in fact be reinforcing in certain situations. You have to understand the context in which they are spoken. For example, many years ago I was walking through a plant with a production superintendent, and he saw an employee with his back to him working on a motor about 50 yards away. The superintendent yelled, "Hey you ole redheaded S. O. B., you better get your rear end to work or I'm going to fire you!" The employee turned, shook his fist at the superintendent, and went back to work. As we walked a little farther, the superintendent turned to me and explained, "If I don't say that to him, he'll come up to me later in the day and say, 'You mad at me or somethin?' He is one of the hardest-working people we've got." It was clear to me that they had a special relationship. Those words written on paper would give the opposite impression of the real relationship.

A touch, a smile, and a gesture can all convey approval. Words are a small part of how we let others know that in our opinion they are doing well.

RULE 4: DON'T USE *BUT* WHEN REINFORCING

Do not reinforce and give corrective feedback at the same time. Separate the correction from the reinforcement by separating them in time. "You did good, but..." is one of the most common errors in attempting to reinforce. People who have a habit of tagging a *but* onto a reinforcer are usually surprised when they learn that people don't see them as being positive. They say, "I tell them all the time that they are doing well." The fact is that they do. The problem is that they don't leave it at that. When they add the qualifier *but,* all the person will remember is what comes after the *but* or, as the person will tell it to others, the criticism. This practice leads to comments such as "No matter what you do, you can never please her" and "He is never satisfied." When giving praise, it is wise to wait until later to give corrective feedback.

Let's say that a new accounting clerk brings you some invoices he has just completed. You look at them and say, "These certainly are neat and look great, but I thought you would be doing 20 an hour by now." It does not take a person with a lot of social sensitivity to know that the net result of this sentence is not positive. It would be much better received if you stopped your comment just before the *but.* Later, you could call on the clerk and say, "I noticed that the last batch of invoices you did was at the rate of 11 per hour. I'll bet if you sorted them by date, you could do even more." If you are guilty of "yes, but," try this simple separation. I think you will be surprised at the reaction you get.

Many children have had the experience of showing good improvement in their school grades only to have a parent say, "I like those four A's, but you are going to have to work harder on that course with the B." As a parent, you could have a much more positive influence on a child's desire to improve if you would congratulate the child on the A's. Later, when the child is getting ready to study, you could say something like, "What do you think you can do to get that B to an A next quarter?"

RULE 5: DON'T ATTEMPT TO REINFORCE AND PUNISH AT THE SAME TIME

This is referred to as the "sandwich method" of punishment. It involves the sandwiching of a punisher between two reinforcers. An example is "John, you are one of the best employees we have ... when you are here. Now, if you don't do something to improve your attendance, we are going to have to let you go. You've got more talent in your little finger than the average person has in her whole body, and that is why I'm so concerned about your attendance record."

Although this is the most common way of teaching managers how to give "negative feedback," it is not recommended for several reasons. First, it is not effective. There is no research showing that this works. It clearly dilutes the punishment. It has been advanced by psychologists as a way of preserving a person's "ego and dignity," but there is no evidence that it does that either. While it may make it easier to deliver a negative message, the positive impact will be totally lost and the corrective message will be diluted.

Second, by pairing reinforcement with punishment, people see the good news as an antecedent for bad news and want to avoid it and you. As soon as you start saying something good, they will start bracing for the bad that will follow.

RULE 6: DON'T REINFORCE AND ASK FOR MORE AT THE SAME TIME

This rule has the same effect as rule 5. "I really liked how quickly and thoroughly you did that last report, and since we're running late with this other report, I'd like you to do it as well." "Sylvia, you are one of the neatest people I know. By the way, would you work for me this weekend?" These attempts at reinforcement are suspect. People would certainly have good reason to doubt their sincerity. When that happens, the reinforcement is lost.

RULE 7: TELL PEOPLE THEY ARE APPRECIATED AND TELL THEM OFTEN

How many times have you heard someone say, "He knows I appreciate his hard work," only to hear the person being discussed say that he wonders if anybody really knows how hard he works. If people are not told overtly and clearly that they are appreciated, they will assume the opposite. A plant manager I know announced early retirement. He said that in the last few years he had lost his enthusiasm for the job and therefore it was time to step aside. His announcement was unexpected. At his retirement party his boss of the last few years told the audience that whenever he had visitors he wanted to impress, he would always bring them to this man's plant. He said he knew that he would always find the plant clean and productive and the employees knowledgeable and friendly. After the dinner the plant manager confided to a friend almost tearfully, "If I had known he felt that way, I wouldn't have retired."

While some people are told occasionally that they are appreciated, the infrequency of the communication can create problems. If we wait too long, their behavior may have deteriorated, and when we finally get around to it, the comment will have a negative effect. The response may be, "It's about time," "You obviously don't appreciate it much," or, as the saying goes, "Too little, too late."

Tell people they are appreciated; tell them clearly and tell them often.

RULE 8: OCCASIONALLY PAIR SOCIAL REINFORCERS WITH A TANGIBLE ITEM THAT ANCHORS A MEMORY

Social reinforcement is a powerful tool. Done correctly, it can improve performance and relationships at the same time. Done incorrectly, it will do the opposite.

The way to make a verbal positive reinforcement memorable and meaningful is to pair it occasionally with a tangible item that will trigger a memory of a desirable behavior. This does not have to be an expensive or elaborate item. I have on my desk an old Indian arrowhead that one of my clients gave me when he told me how much he valued our training. It may not be worth much monetarily, but it means a great deal to me professionally and personally. But keep in mind that the positive reinforcement does not reside in the object. It resides in the memory of the event and the story it gives me to tell. Conversely, the office manager who gruffly presents his star employee with an award she has earned for improved performance reduces the probability that his opinion or presence will be valued in the future. You can be sure that the story she will tell about it will not be a positive one, and the award will be devalued as a result.

RULE 9: GIVE PEOPLE THE OPPORTUNITY TO RELIVE THEIR ACCOMPLISHMENT

Many times when people do good things, you are not there to see them. You usually just see the results. By asking people how they accomplished something, you give them an acceptable way to talk about what they did; how persistent they were, how disciplined they were, or how resourceful they were.

We call this reliving of an accomplishment a celebration. You can celebrate an accomplishment with one person or with a thousand. The one question, "How'd you do that?" can do more to increase positive reinforcement in a relationship than any other thing you can say or ask.

RULE 10: NEVER FORCE A TENTH RULE JUST TO HAVE 10 RULES WHEN YOU REALLY ONLY HAVE 9

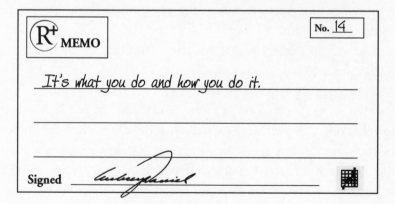

R^+ MEMO   No. 14

It's what you do and how you do it.

Signed

15 RECEIVING REINFORCEMENT
What to Do When You Get It and What to Do When You Don't

You can tell the character of every man
when you see how he receives praise.

—SENECA
Epistles

How you receive reinforcement has a significant effect on how much you get. If you want to receive more reinforcement, you must reinforce the behavior of reinforcing. Many people complain about not being appreciated when the fact is that attempts to reinforce them have been met with punishment. Why would anyone punish someone who is attempting to reinforce? It is certainly not intentional; it is another case of unintended consequences.

Have you ever tried to compliment someone on her choice of clothes only to have her say, "Oh, these old rags?" I'm often tempted to say in response, "Well, I guess that just shows my poor taste in clothing." Are you familiar with the following scenario? The woman says, "You never tell me you love me." The man responds, "I love you!" "You don't mean it," she replies.

I witnessed this scene many times while working as a marital therapist. What do you think the wife has done to the probability that her husband will increase the frequency of telling her that he loves her? When I pointed out this problem to my patients, the wife usually responded, "He only said that because of what I said. If I have to ask him, it doesn't mean as much. He ought to think of it on his own."

The problem is that if he doesn't think of it on his own, how can his wife get him to do it? She should start by reinforcing every attempt he makes to compliment her. If she prompts him and he responds by saying, "I love you," she should simply accept his comments as sincere and respond positively. If he is punished every time he tries, he will never think of saying it on his own.

YOUR REINFORCEMENT IS YOUR RESPONSIBILITY: WHAT TO DO WHEN YOU GET IT

If you don't get the reinforcement you need from others or from your environment, you are the one who is affected the most. If you feel you don't get the reinforcement and recognition you deserve, look first at how you have been reinforcing those who reinforce you. Reinforcing is a behavior like any other behavior. If you make people feel uncomfortable or in some other way inadvertently punish their attempts at reinforcement, you can't expect them to continue doing it.

In the psychologist Robert Mager's film *Who Did What To Whom* there is a vignette where the boss is saying, "I was able to get you a 5 percent salary increase." The woman sitting in front of his desk slams her notepad on the desk and says, "You call *that* a raise?" Then she leaves in a huff.

She was obviously disappointed by the amount of the raise, but was that a productive thing for her to do? In addition to how such a reaction might affect day-to-day working relationships in the present, do you think her reaction will cause the boss to work harder to get her a raise in the future?

ADA consultant Jamie Daniels was consulting in a battery plant where there was a very contentious relationship between labor and management. As part of the training, the supervisors saw a movie about a ranch foreman out west who was having trouble with the ranch hands. The cook, the behavioral guru, was advising the foreman to try positive reinforcement rather than the usual negative reinforcement and punishment. To reward the foreman for changing his management style, the cook baked him some of his favorite blueberry muffins.

Later in the day after watching the film, a supervisor walked into Jamie's office, sat down, and said woefully, "I just handed out my first 'blueberry muffin.'" "How did it go?" Jamie asked. "Well, I walked up to this employee on the line and said, 'Jack, I really appreciate the increased effort you put out last week.' He looked at me like I was crazy and said, 'What the devil are you talking about?' Then I responded, 'Your efficiency was up 17 percent last week, and I really appreciate it.' He then turned to walk away and said, 'Why don't you save that BS for someone who gives a flip?'" Jamie had a tough time getting that supervisor to try reinforcing again.

Max, the vice president of the textile mill we mentioned earlier, confided to the behavioral expert Courtney Mills that he never saw anything to positively reinforce in his cost meetings. As was noted before, those meetings were notorious for their negativity. Courtney said that he would sit in on the meeting and signal Max when he saw something that Max should comment on. Within the first 15 minutes Max had made 10 attempts to reinforce at Courtney's prompting. In the last hour and 15 minutes he made no attempts even though Courtney was signaling him to do so.

Courtney, realizing what had happened, asked the supervisors and managers to stay after Max left. He explained to them that it was obvious that they were not reinforcing Max's attempts at reinforcing since he stopped early in the meeting. One by one they explained that when Max said something positive about their cost data, it surprised them so much that all they could do was stammer and continue on. They related that they didn't know what to say. Their responses made Max nervous, since this was also new for him. Their discomfort was punishing enough to Max to stop his new, reinforcing behavior quickly. Courtney rehearsed them on responding to a reinforcer from Max by simply saying thank you.

Another example is provided by Paul, the owner of a furniture company, who gave a surprise bonus after a particularly successful year. The amount of the bonus was approximately a million dollars! Out of 7000 employees, how many people took the time to write or call Paul to thank him? The answer is an astonishing zero. How many do you think took the time to call or write to complain? Over 100. How many times do you think he has done that again? If you guessed "none," you would be correct. How many times would you do it? I was bothered by the lack of response to Paul, particularly since I felt partially responsible. Later in the year I was doing some survey work in his company, and at the end of the session I asked the groups, "Do you remember the bonus you got on New Year's Day?" In one of the groups a woman shouted out, "God, did it!" I said, "I don't understand." She continued, "I spent too much money for Christmas, and I prayed to God to please help me out. I came to work on New Year's Day, and it was the answer to my prayers." I said, "I'm sure you thanked God, but did you thank Paul?" Her answer floored me. She said, "Could I do that?"

Why do people need permission in business to thank someone when they don't need permission to criticize? There certainly is a problem in business with reinforcing up the chain of command. There are all sorts of descriptions of people who do that, and none of them are complimentary. We talk of apple-polishing, brownnosing, and sucking up.

The boss's behavior is subject to the same laws of behavior that apply to everyone else. If management's attempts to improve the workplace go unreinforced, you can bet that there will be fewer of them.

We seem to have a cultural problem with receiving reinforcement. Most people have been taught not to "toot their own horn," and this has resulted in people demeaning their accomplishments or making self-effacing comments such as "It was nothing," "I was just lucky," and "Even a blind hog finds an acorn sometimes." I complimented a woman on her hair once, and she said, "I can't do a thing with it. I think I'm going to have it all cut off." So much for what I know about hair! For many people an "Aw, shucks" is about as close as they can come to accepting reinforcement publicly.

Reinforcement for many people at work comes so infrequently that they don't know how to take it. When I attempt to reinforce busboys in restaurants, maids in hotels, and others who do not get a lot of reinforcement from the public, more often than not it appears to embarrass them or make them uncomfortable. I teach people that if they don't know what to say when they are reinforced, a simple thank-you is quite adequate.

Janis Allen, the author of *I Saw What You Did and I Know Who You Are*, tells the story of a manager who delivered little positive reinforcement and almost never interacted with his employees unless there was a problem or he needed something. In class he realized that he needed to use positive reinforcement. Janis relates the following about his first attempt:

> *The next morning he came in and said, "I tried to reinforce and, oh boy, what a horrible experience." He had returned to his office and discovered that his secretary, Lisa, had voluntarily taken on and completed a rather time-consuming project. Although he had mentioned the project to Lisa, he didn't ask her to do it. Yet, she had taken the initiative to crunch the numbers, separate the information for each supervisor, and write a cover letter for his approval and signature. She had saved him many hours of work.*
>
> *Alex picked up the letter, marched to Lisa's desk and said, "I just saw this report you wrote and this letter is excellent. You have saved me considerable time here and I appreciate it. I didn't know you knew precisely what I wanted, but this is exactly how I would have done it. This is great!"*
>
> *Lisa's reaction? A blank stare.*
>
> *The silence finally became unbearable for Alex, so he turned quickly to run to the safety of his office. As he started to duck through the door Lisa said, "Alex, what did you really come out here for?"*[1]

Lisa couldn't believe that he came to her desk just to tell her that he appreciated her good work. It obviously was not a daily occurrence.

However, because he was not comfortable with social reinforcement, her response was instrumental in determining whether he would do it again. She didn't intend to make him uncomfortable, but she did, reducing the probability that he would reinforce her again or would do it to others.

WHAT TO DO WHEN YOU DON'T GET THE REINFORCEMENT YOU NEED OR DESERVE

I remember an occasion many years ago at Georgia Regional Hospital when the psychology department was doing some things that were producing dramatic results in the treatment units. I sent my boss, the hospital superintendent, a memo about the program and the results it was achieving. A couple of weeks went by, and I received no reply. I started pouting. I thought to myself, "He doesn't care about what we are doing. I guess I ought to be like everybody else in the system and just put in the time. Nobody appreciates anything you do around here."

Fortunately, when I was in his office one day talking to his secretary, the superintendent walked in. I asked, "Dr. B, what did you think about that memo I sent you a couple of weeks ago?" "What memo?" he replied. I told him, and he said, "I don't remember it. Let me see if I can find it." We walked into his office, and he started looking in his in-basket which was piled about a foot high. He sorted down about 2 weeks' worth and finally said, "Is this it?" I nodded. "Tell me about it," he said.

When I explained it to him, he got excited and said, "I need to tell Dr. Bush [his boss] about this. I think he would be very impressed. He could use this in his meeting with the governor next week." I felt badly that I had thought he didn't care, but it taught me something: What is at the top of my agenda is not necessarily at the top of others' agendas. It wasn't that he didn't care. He just had too many other things that were pressing on him. I thought no response meant he didn't care. In fact, he cared a great deal.

Years ago my wife, Becky, got on my case about my clothes: I didn't hang them up. I had a bad habit of leaving them on chairs, closet doors, and the floor. She would nag me and say, "You'd think a grown man would hang up his clothes. You certainly set a poor example for Laura-Lee and Joanna."

Since she was making such a big deal out of this, one day I decided that no piece of clothing that touched my body would touch the floor. I was going to put all my clothes in their place *every* time I pulled them off.

For 2 weeks I was perfect. Guess what she said to me about it? Not one word. Righteous indignation began to fill my soul. I began to think of what I was going to say to her: "When my clothes are on the floor, it's a big deal, but when they are hanging in the closet, it's no deal at all. Right?" I imagined the look on her face. I knew she would not have a comeback because God was on my side now. I wanted to ambush her with this so that I would catch her when she least expected it. That way the confrontation would have the greatest impact on her.

One day when she was in the kitchen I leaned on the kitchen counter and said quietly, "Have you noticed anything unusual about my clothes lately?" "Yes, I have," she said. "I have been meaning to say something to you about it. You have been doing great. It really has helped me keep the house clean. Thank you so much." Talk about deflated. Who would have expected that? I felt ashamed about all the thoughts I had had about her not caring.

These two situations stand out in my memory because they taught me a lesson: No response does not necessarily mean no caring. I've learned that if I don't get a response to something I have done that I feel is noteworthy, I should ask for it.

There are all kinds of ways to ask for reinforcement. Some are appropriate, and some are annoying and irritating and create an effect that is the opposite of what you want. There is a fine line between asking and demanding. We have all known people who "constantly need reassurance." We usually hate to see them coming. Some seem to beg for reinforcement, and some demand it. At some time you have been put in a situation where you felt that you had to say something complimentary even when you did not want to, but because of the demands of the social situation, you did it anyway.

There are ways to ask for reinforcement that do not turn people off. Usually you can ask a question such as "Did you see the report I turned in last week?" You should not ask, "Did you *like* the report I turned in last week?" That pressures the average person, and you will usually get a response out of obligation rather than sincerity.

OOHING AND AHHING

I have developed what I call "oohing and ahhing" with my family. Since I know the effects of reinforcement on behavior, I know that if I don't get enough of it at certain times, it will affect my performance.

One summer day I decided to start on a yard project I had put off for many weeks. I had promised my wife that I would line the walk with bricks to make a nice edge for the flower beds and give it a finished look. It was a hard job, and the day was hot.

I had been working for a couple of hours or so, and I began to have impulses to quit, thinking that I had done enough for one day. My back hurt, my hands were sore, and sweat was pouring off my body. However, I knew that if I left the job for another day, the winter snow would cover the bricks in the middle of the sidewalk before I got around to finishing it.

I set a goal of finishing up to a certain crack in the sidewalk. When I reached that point, I would try to get some oohing and ahhing. When I got to that crack, I went to the back door, stuck my head in, and yelled, "Hey. Somebody! I need some oohing and ahhing out here." Becky yelled back, "I'll be there in a minute." I went back to the sidewalk, and when she came out, she said exactly the right thing. "How did you get those bricks so straight?" she asked. "That's going to look great." I said, "Thanks. You can go back in the house. I think I can finish now." And I did.

GIVE MORE OF IT

People who get reinforcement reinforce others more often. You increase the chance that you will be reinforced by reinforcing others. Levin and Isen conducted several studies on the variables that influence "helping behavior."[2] In one study a woman involved in the experiment entered a telephone booth and pretended to make a telephone call. Before leaving, she placed a coin in the coin return and picked up some papers but purposely left a letter that was addressed but had no stamp. The experimenters wanted to see if finding the coin would have any effect on whether a person would buy a stamp and mail the letter. Since the letter was addressed to the experimenter, they were able to learn the exact percentage of people who did so. The results amazed me. Among the people who found the money, 88 percent mailed the letter. Among the people who did not find the money, only 10 percent mailed it.

In a similar study a woman bumped into a person as he or she left the telephone booth, spilling her papers on the sidewalk. The researchers found that 91 percent of the people who found the money helped her pick the papers up and only 11 percent of those who did not find the money helped her.

In a Ford plant where we did some consulting work an assembly-line worker had made good improvement in his work and had been reinforced frequently by his boss. One day he called the boss over and said, "Next time you are in the tooling department, tell that machinist over there he is doing a good job on the dogleg. I have been keeping a graph, and the number of good ones has really gone up." His boss said, "Why don't you tell him? Let's go over there." As the two of them appeared in the next department, the tooling shop manager saw them coming, turned to one of his supervisors, and said, "Here they come; get ready for a fight." To the manager's surprise, the assembly-line worker approached him and said he wanted to tell one of his machinists what a good job he was doing. The manager then stepped back and watched the two employees looking at the graph and talking about the machinist's good work. When the manager told me the story later, he paused and said, "You know, watching those two guys poring over that graph and talking seriously about their job performance was really something. I got kind of choked up."

Tom, an older employee in a fiber plant, performed significantly above all the other operators in the department. He got lots of reinforcement from his supervisor. As the supervisor began to use positive reinforcement with the rest of the shift, others began to make significant improvements. One day one of the newer employees actually outperformed Tom. When Tom learned about it, he called the supervisor over and said, "You better go over there and let that guy know he is really doing well."

As you can see, people who get reinforced reinforce others more often. When you reinforce others, you increase the chance that you will get reinforced. As Jerrold Jennings, former personnel manager at Milliken & Co., said, "Positive reinforcement is contagious."

SELF-REINFORCEMENT IS A SMART STRATEGY

While you are waiting for others to notice how smart you are, what magnificent things you have accomplished, or the small improvements you have made in some behavior, you can arrange your environment in ways that will provide you with self-reinforcement. Samuel Butler wrote, "The advantage of self-praise is that you can lay it on in just the right places and in the right amount."

When I started jogging, I knew that I would need lots of reinforcement. Running had never been one of my favorite things; therefore, I knew I had to change my environment to produce consequences for running and not running. First, I found several friends who were running and set times to run with them. That way I would be less likely to back out at the last minute. Second, I charted my distances and times and put the graphs on the wall of my office. This way people would see them and ask me about my running. If I was doing well, the questions were positively reinforcing. If I was not doing well, the questions and comments were negatively reinforcing. In both cases they got me out on the road.

A coworker, Jerry Pounds, and I made a bet that we would finish the Peachtree Road Race in Atlanta on July 4 in 55 minutes or less or forfeit $250 to our least favorite charity. The check was to be mailed by my secretary on July 5 if we did not show up with a T-shirt from the race. Knowledge of the bet generated lots of conversation in the office and provided enough reinforcement to keep us training. Needless to say, we both finished the race. Negative reinforcement got us running, but it has been positive reinforcement that has kept us running these many years.

Whether losing weight, quitting smoking, or getting more done around the house or at work, taking the initiative to involve friends and family members in your reinforcement plan is a good idea.

REINTERPRET YOUR SITUATION

I had a friend who left his job of many years to go into business on his own. The business was not doing well, and he was struggling to keep it going. He and his family lived on a small farm south of the city, and early one December his wife asked him several times to go cut a Christmas tree from the nearby woods. One day, after his wife had asked him again, he reluctantly agreed to do it. He took his young son along, and the family dog decided to tag along as well. My friend was grumpy from worrying about all the problems he was facing, not knowing how he would solve them. He was somewhat irritated at his son's many questions as well as the dog's barking. After looking for a long time for just the right tree, he finally cut one and started home.

As he cleared the woods and started walking across the field to the house, he looked toward the house and saw the light on in the kitchen as the afternoon was turning into dusk. He knew that his wife was cooking supper. He saw smoke curling from the chimney, and he knew that there was a fire in the fireplace in the den. His young son was skipping happily along, and the dog was running back and forth as the man dragged the tree across the field. Suddenly it hit him. Here he was harassing himself about all his problems, and he was in the middle of a scene straight out of Currier and Ives. This was what the season was all about, and he was missing it.

That story had particular meaning to me because at the time I was traveling a lot and it seemed that there was always a problem. Either the plane was late, the reservations were wrong, or the weather was bad. I was in a chronically foul mood. As I listened to my friend tell his story, it occurred to me that no one was making me travel. This was the way I chose to make my living. I could make myself miserable, or I could make the most of it. It was my choice. Rather than keep myself upset about the trials and tribulations of travel, I decided to use the time to see what reinforcers I could get while en route. I began to watch people to see examples of behavioral interactions that I could use in my seminars. I bought a laptop computer so that I could write while waiting for flights and during flights. I tried to learn something about the geography and history of the places where I was going. I used the time to read articles that I did not have time to read otherwise. Not only were these activities helpful in improving my attitude about travel, I increased my productivity at the same time.

Your reinforcement is your responsibility—no one else's. If you don't get it, you are the one who suffers. By using the techniques in this chapter, you should be able to get the reinforcement you need to strengthen the behaviors that will serve you and those you care about in a positive way.

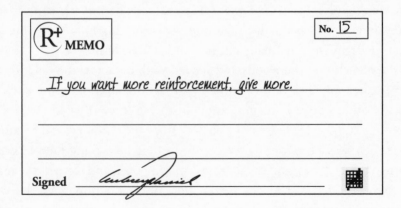

R⁺ MEMO

No. 15

If you want more reinforcement, give more.

Signed _____

16 DELIBERATE ACTS OF REINFORCEMENT

I asked why somebody doesn't do something,
and then I realized I am somebody.

—SIGN ON MY WALL

IT'S ABOUT YOU

I hope that by now you understand the title of this book. It is really about changing *your* behavior. Mark Twain's quote at the beginning of Chap. 2 was obviously tongue in cheek. It is certainly easier for all of us to see the faults of others than to see our own. This has been noted throughout history. The Bible says to remove the beam in your own eye before attempting to remove the mote in your neighbor's. To paraphrase Shakespeare in *Julius Caesar*, "The fault, dear Brutus, is not in our stars, but in ourselves." Or as Pogo says "We have met the enemy, and he is us.

We create many of our own problems by the way we behave toward others. Therefore, to change the behavior of others, we must first change how we relate to them. By now you realize that the most effective way to change another person is to use positive reinforcement. You will henceforth need to change the frequency of your reinforcement, the timing of it, and the nature of it to be most effective. On a recent business trip to Asia I heard one Asian businessperson and government official after another talk about the economic future of their countries. They ultimately talked about changing the behavior of leaders in government and business. Unfortunately, most of them talked about changing the behavior of those people through negative consequences. By now not only are you convinced that there is a better way, you know how to go about it.

ONE PERSON ALWAYS MAKES A DIFFERENCE

Most people, even after reading this book, don't realize the tremendous power they have to bring about changes in society. I know many people who single-handedly have brought about profound changes in the lives of thousands of families. The saying "One person *can* make a difference" should be changed to "One person *always* makes a difference."

Chaos theory has shown that even small changes in our environment can make huge changes when they are iterated many times. When a single individual is reinforced for a positive change in his behavior, he changes what he does in relation to others. This changes them, and as a result of their behavior change, they change others. And so it goes in an unending pattern. The question is not "Can I make a difference?" but "What *kind* of difference will I make?" If you see someone go out of her way to help another person and you do nothing to provide reinforcement for the helper, you shouldn't complain that "people don't seem to care about each other like they used to." If you receive outstanding service in a store and you say or do nothing to reinforce that behavior, don't say, "All anybody seems to care about anymore is the paycheck." If you don't thank someone who lets you merge into the line of traffic at an entrance ramp on the expressway, don't get upset when no one lets you in the next time. While each of these things seems trivial in the face of the world's problems, when practiced daily by many people, they can have a significant impact on every part of society. The techniques discussed in this book are very powerful no matter who applies them or where they are applied.

JUST DO IT!

Dr. Jon Bailey, a professor of psychology at Florida State University, begins every session of his performance management classes by having his students recite in unison: "I can make a difference." And they do! As a requirement of the class, each student has to find a local business to apply what he or she has learned. Believe it or not, these students have designed and implemented projects that over the years have saved local businesses and government agencies millions of dollars. From restaurants and construction businesses to local and state governments, they have tackled problems of customer service, sales, quality, and productivity. Think about it. They change a business when they have no authority to do so. They have made significant changes even when given little support by managers because the techniques they use are compelling and effective.

Every day I talk to people who have made significant changes in their families, companies, and communities. The even better news is that most of them become passionate about helping others do the same.

A retired army officer called me last year. He told me that he had read one of my books and, since he had spent some time in Bosnia, wondered if this approach could get the Serbs and Croats to work together in Bosnia. Of course, I answered that it could. He now has a Fulbright scholarship and is on the faculty at the University of Sarejevo, where he plans to teach a course in performance management.

A man who retired from a U. S. oil company wanted to translate one of my books into Turkish because he saw significant benefit for his native country. I could list many others who are doing similar things.

It is unfortunate that people think they have to have a position of some formal influence to make significant changes. They think they have to be in politics or in a leadership position in a company or civic organization. When students ask me about how to get a job where they can apply what they have learned, my response is to get a job, any job, and start doing it the first day. Do it at home. Do it on the way to work.

Do it at work and on the way home. Do it in the mall, with your friends, with everyone you meet. As the sports shoe commercial says, "Just do it."

FOUR TO ONE

Years ago I introduced a concept to business that I called 4 to 1. The concept was based on some research done by Professors C. H. Madsen and C. R. Madsen at Florida State University in which they investigated effective teacher behavior.[1] They discovered that teachers who had well-disciplined and high-achieving students had positive reinforcement rates roughly four times their punishment rates. Teachers who had rates less than 4 to 1 had classrooms with both discipline and achievement problems. Stuart found similar results in comparing parents who had nondelinquent children and those who had delinquent ones.[2] As was already mentioned, Risley found that professional and working-class parents had rates of reinforcement that were four or more times their rate of negative verbal interactions.

We taught managers to track their positive and negative interactions and try to achieve a ratio of at least four positive reinforcers to one punisher. Before the training, the best ratios were in the range of 1:2. That is, they had twice as many negative interactions with employees as positives. (Risley's data showed that welfare parents had the same ratio.) However, once they began to track their behavior and scan their environment for things to positively reinforce, they began to find more and more opportunities. Ratios of 20 to 1 or higher were soon common. This simple change in supervisory behavior often led to dramatic changes in performance in the workplace.

What do you think would happen in your company, family, or community if you started to do this and got others to do the same thing? Think of the impact on society if everybody did this. It would mean that daily interactions would be overwhelmingly positive. People would be spending most of their time concentrating on what was going right. This would cause people to approach problems in a different way, trying to find constructive solutions rather than finding fault.

YOUR NEIGHBOR'S KEEPER

Sy Zivan, an executive with Xerox, was visiting the company's facilities in Japan. As he and his Japanese guide were waiting for a train, Sy noticed a janitor working on a spot on the floor about the size of a dime. He saw the janitor scrub the spot to no avail. He went back to his supply cart and got another cleaner and tried again. He failed again, only to return to his supplies to get something else so that he could scrub some more. Finally he was successful. As he was putting up his equipment to move to another area, Sy commented to his Japanese guide how impressed he was with the man's industriousness. He said that in the United States, a janitor probably would have hit that spot with a broom, and if it didn't come up, he would have left it and moved on. At that point the guide excused himself from Sy and went over to talk to the janitor. After a few seconds of conversation the janitor turned to Sy and started talking and bowing. Sy, not knowing what was happening, started bowing back. This went on for several bows till the man resumed working. When he left, Sy asked the guide what that had been about. The guide told him that he had thanked the man for doing his job in such an exemplary manner that he had impressed his foreign visitor. In other words, he took it as his responsibility to make sure that that behavior did not go unnoticed. Make other people's *good behavior* your business. Let no good deed go unreinforced.

DELIBERATE ACTS OF REINFORCEMENT

Make it your business to positively reinforce behavior that does not effect you directly every day. I am taking it for granted that you are ready to reinforce the behavior of those who do things that affect you directly. Now I want you to scan your environment to see things that people do that match your values but don't necessarily affect you at that moment. Try to increase your reinforcement for those behaviors.

CHANGING THE WAY THE WORLD WORKS

The mission of our company is to "change the way the world works." It may not be as difficult as you think. Changing the world is no more difficult than changing your own behavior. If you have learned to change your behavior, you know how to change the world. You do it one behavior at a time.

A book by R. M. Axelrod, *The Evolution of Cooperation,* has in it some advice that may help you create opportunities for deliberate acts of kindness.[3] In doing research on how people come to cooperate, he discovered that those who are effective in creating conditions of cooperation do the following:

1. Always assume cooperation
2. Reinforce any act of cooperation
3. Do not reinforce any act of noncooperation
4. Are quick to forgive noncooperative acts

In his research Axelrod discovered that this approach was so powerful that it took only 5 percent of any group who practiced it to change the behavior of the rest of the group.

You probably represent much more than 5 percent of the group that is important to you, and it's obvious that there has never been a better time to make positive reinforcement your consequence of choice. Begin to do your part. Put down this book and find some behavior that you would like to see more of and positively reinforce it now! Let me know what happens. I know you will make a difference. You can't avoid it. H. G. Wells stated it profoundly: "Every individual without exception changes the species, and its contribution is permanent so long as the species endures."[4]

Now that you know how to change behavior, you can make sure that you will change our species—our world—for the better. Remember, you change other people's habits by first changing your own.

> **R⁺ MEMO**
>
> No. 16
>
> *You create your future by what you reinforce today.*
>
> Signed _____

APPENDIX

BEING A SELF-MANAGER: IT'S YOU VERSUS YOU.[1]

Gail Snyder

B. F. Skinner, inventor, author, and the man known as the creator of behavioral science, arranged the details of his life down to the order of the books on his desktop. Those he arranged in such a way that he could grab the volume he needed without taking his eyes off the work at hand. "He didn't do this because he was compulsive," explained Robert Epstein, Ph.D. "Far from it. He did it because he knew if the behavioral chain was too long, the effort too great to pull down a certain book, he just wouldn't do it." According to Epstein, Skinner's fellow researcher and friend, B. F. Skinner was the epitome of a self-manager. Indeed, he managed his life so succinctly that he scheduled time for leisure (a part of life he felt crucial to his own creativity) and put the finishing touches on a manuscript only hours before his death in 1990.

"He was a self-manager because it changed the probabilities of all kinds of behaviors that were important to him. It made it easy and effortless for him to be productive and creative," said Epstein. Epstein believes that B.F. Skinner's abilities to self-manage were also self-taught and in that there is a lesson for all of us. That lesson is that we, too, can become self-managers.

"Self-managers can cope with changing worlds because they are not dependent on their Daytimer," explained Epstein. "They have skills that help them through changing environments."

These days entire sections of bookstores are set aside for self-management books. The study of self-management is not a new idea. It has been researched, written, and read about for over 25 years. Yet Epstein compares the effects of much of the literature on this subject to the old adage: "Give a man a fish and you feed him for a day; teach a man to fish and you've fed him for a lifetime." "Self-management is a different way to live your life," he said. To guide people toward that life change, Epstein developed three functionally distinct, self-management skill categories, what he calls the Three M's of Self-Management:

1. MODIFY YOUR ENVIRONMENT.

We do things every day to change our environment, but we do not look at these things in terms of self-management. For example, we write ourselves notes as reminders, set an alarm clock to wake ourselves up, and tie strings around our fingers to remember to remember. According to Epstein, the problem with these types of cues to modify our behavior is that we do them in a fit of desperation rather than as a targeted effort at self-management. When we consciously change our environment to modify our behavior, we will eventually come up with the right change. "There are hundreds of changes you can make, but you only have to make one to dramatically change the probability [of a behavior]," said Epstein. "For example, when Skinner stuck a television on top of his exercise bike, he was simply changing his environment to promote a desired behavior."

We can also change our environment by making changes in our bodies, such as practicing stress control by using methods such as biofeedback. "Modifying your environment could include a whole slew of relaxation techniques for modifying your internal environment," he said. How does one get himself to start a new behavior? Epstein suggests trying another behavior, one that is easier than the behavior you are trying to encourage or change. For example, if you bite your nails, buy reams of nail files and place them everywhere, including in your pockets. Then, when you get the urge to bite, file instead.

2. MONITOR YOUR BEHAVIOR.

"Anytime you heighten your awareness of a behavior, you behave better," said Epstein. "That will work in both directions, getting rid of undesirable behavior or strengthening desirable behavior." The trick here is to make the monitoring process as effortless as possible. Keeping track of your performance does not have to be restricted to pencil and paper data or formal graphs. If you keep count in your head and it works for you, that is fine. Some people make small tears in their cigarette packages to monitor how many they have smoked. You can fill in dots on a page, tear the edges of a piece of paper, or drop pennies or tokens in a jar. The key in monitoring yourself is that you set up a process that is so easy you do not have to think about it, one that is natural and fun to do.

"I will make an assertion that the people who exercise, keep their weight under control, and are productive are self-managers whether they know it or not," said Epstein. "If you carefully observe how they conduct themselves during the day, you'll find that they do these things even when they have never heard of them."

The weigh-ins of weight loss programs, the batting statistics of a baseball player, and the handicap of a golfer are all means of making people more aware of their performance. Epstein asserts that there is no such animal as self-reinforcement, that a self-reinforcing person is essentially a self-monitoring person. "What you have really done is heightened your awareness of what it is you have accomplished," he said. "Many studies show that if you get someone to be more aware of what they are doing, they'll be better at it, virtually without exception."

3. MAKE A COMMITMENT.

If you have ever told someone, "I'll be there at four o'clock. You can count on me," you have made a commitment. Making a commitment highly increases the probability that you will follow through on a behavior. That is why this category of self-management may be the most difficult. "You can use making a commitment to deliberately and systematically change your behavior," explained Epstein. "Not just on random occasions."

An extreme example of making a commitment is to write a nasty letter to your manager, sign it, seal it, and give it to a friend with a statement such as, "If I smoke another cigarette, drop this in the mail." You have then set up a negative, immediate, and certain consequence for yourself. A less risky means of doing this is to write a check to your least favorite charity and give it to your friend under similar contingencies.

Have trouble getting yourself to work on time? Epstein suggests you set off a time bomb; no, not to blow yourself out of bed, but to set up a commitment that you are compelled to follow through on. During college he hid an alarm clock in the library shelves set to go off at 9:00 a.m. On the back of the alarm clock he taped his name, phone number, and address. "I did this all through graduate school," he said. "That example is a bit extreme, but you can use it to push yourself the extra mile if you really need that push. Set up real contingencies involving other people."

One may try many things in each of these categories before hitting on just the right formula for individual successful self-management. However, the skills themselves will definitely work if followed diligently. "Behavior changes behavior, and that is what we need to know," explained Epstein. "You know about these principles, because you use some of them as managers of other people. Use them on yourself. When you manage others, you can screw up. The fact is that makes us a little bit too timid because of the consequences that may follow our decisions. But in self-management, it's you versus you. When you practice these skills you either come up even or you come up ahead. You can't really come up behind. It's fun—management without the risk."

LEARNING TO LEARN WITH PM²

Gail Snyder

Stephanie Janoulis is just like any other 10-year-old girl. She loves clothes and likes to ride her bike. Her role model is Joan Collins of *Dynasty* (the television series) fame. But Stephanie has a neuropsychological deficit. In layman's terms, Stephanie can learn, but her mind forgets where it stores the data, making it difficult for her to retrieve the information from her memory bank. Compounded with this learning disability is the fact that Stephanie is slightly hyperactive.

The Janoulises became aware of Stephanie's problem when she entered prekindergarten. "My child has been tested everywhere from Augusta, Georgia, to Birmingham, Alabama," said Stephen Janoulis, Stephanie's father. Unfortunately, the diagnoses were as varied as the testing locations, ranging from ineducably mentally retarded to emotionally disturbed. "One teacher told us, 'There is nothing wrong with your daughter. She's just plain lazy,'" said Janoulis. Today, Steve and his wife, Prissy, have traced the beginning of Stephanie's problems to an incident that occurred when she was 3 years old. While playing, she badly injured a finger and had to be anesthetized for reconstructive surgery. Several doctors told the Janoulises that in all probability, she was overanesthetized, causing her present learning disabilities.

But getting to the root of the problem only explained the reason for the disability, not how to deal with it. Stephanie and her parents needed a way to make learning and studying a rewarding experience. Steve Janoulis explained, "Study time was a horror. She'd ask us how to spell a word. We'd tell her, and 2 minutes later she'd ask again how to spell the same word. She knew she had a problem, and it was extremely frustrating for her."

A year ago, Janoulis, whose college background is, ironically, in special education, attended a two-and-a-half day Performance Management seminar along with several of his Georgia Power associates. Although he definitely saw PM's applicable possibilities at work, he couldn't help but think about his daughter's problems as he listened.

He explained, "Two weeks before I went to PM training, it was suggested that we take our daughter to a school for learning-disabled children. These are the children with very, very serious personal problems. That, I think, was the lowest point that my wife and I had ever reached."

He went home and told his wife about the PM process. "When I went to Dr. Daniels's class, he was talking about pinpoints, and that is probably the key thing that helped us with our daughter—learning to be specific about problems and performance. All of these specialists had talked in generalities but had never gotten down to the specifics," he said.

One psychiatrist had suggested that Stephanie might have a neuropsychological deficit, but the tests had not verified that theory. Janoulis decided to take what he had learned so far at PM training and apply it to studying his daughter's behavior. "I got out the graph paper and started to keep track of how long my daughter could do a task. I selected watching television, because every child loves to watch television. I found out that she could only sit down and watch television for 5 minutes at a time, at the longest. She would forget what she was watching, but she could recall it later."

He then asked her teacher for all of her spelling scores, reasoning that spelling was a subject that Stephanie did consistently at school, so he would have no problem collecting data. " I started plotting out her spelling grades and established a baseline. Then I made a costly mistake," laughed Janoulis.

He promised his daughter that she could buy a new item of clothing for every A she made in spelling. "I figured that the child just doesn't make A's and it would be something special for her to achieve and go for," he explained.

Stephanie brought home three As that first week. For a 10-year-old she had expensive tastes, and for Janoulis the experience was a pocket-book punisher. "I figured, 'Well, I can't afford to put my child through school this way. I'd better regroup,'" he said.

Janoulis gathered all of his data and called a meeting with Stephanie's teacher, her special education teacher, her tutor, the school psychiatrist, and a private psychiatrist. He shared the data that he had collected on Stephanie's grades and attention span. One of the things that his grade graph made apparent was that Stephanie's scores didn't go up and down as erratically when she took medication, something that would have possibly gone unnoticed if Janoulis had not collected the data.

With the use of this information, the psychiatrists were able to confirm the diagnosis of a neuropsychological deficit and also the fact that Stephanie had hand-eye coordination problems. "We all got our heads together and tried the team approach," said Janoulis. "I told them that I would like to use the Performance Management process and talked to them briefly about what it was. Her special education teacher then decided to use behavioral methods."

Next, Janoulis attended the 2-week Performance Management training session. "Thank God for the 2-week course!" he stated. "I knew this process would be great for my daughter."

Janoulis decided to break down each of Stephanie's subjects into small tasks so that Stephanie could recognize small improvements and so that he could positively reinforce her more often. He used contingencies, based on the Premack principle. Discovered by Dr. David Premack through his laboratory research, the principle states: "If you make something a person does often contingent on doing something you want them to do more often, then the behavior you want will increase in frequency."

"It works wonders!" said Janoulis. "Also, we could reinforce her with 'ooh and ah' sessions, hand clapping, or a special treat involving social things. I learned real fast to keep my reinforcers cheap."

Because of her hand-eye coordination problems, Stephanie could not use repetitive writing as a means of memorization. For example, writing a word many times did not help her learn its spelling. But Janoulis found that she could learn by using oral repetition. "The flashcards that Dr. Daniels uses are a perfect solution to that," said Janoulis.

He and his wife used index cards with questions on one side and answers on the back. They made the cards for both Stephanie and their 8-year-old son, Jason, who does not have a learning disability. Both children use the cards with their junior Trivial Pursuit board game. "Both of my children now play Trivial Pursuit with their homework. They enjoy that," he explained.

Before this new method of studying, Stephanie had become over-whelmed when she looked at all of the things she needed to learn. To make learning fun and less intimidating, her parents wrote down one question or fact per flashcard. For example, in a subject such as geogra-phy, one card said, "Define an ocean." Another card asked, "How many oceans are there?" Learning the facts one step at a time didn't appear as such an obstacle to Stephanie, and each flashcard represented an opportunity for reinforcement.

Janoulis also purchased a computer, which helped Stephanie with her hand-eye coordination. He went from computer store to computer store in search of instructional programs that provided immediate positive reinforcement for correct answers. He finally found a game for learning math that provided immediate R+. As for the reinforcement schedule that he provides, he admitted, "I've started a variable ratio schedule with Stephanie, because some nights I'm just too tired to help her."

Steve and Prissy recently met with Stephanie's special education teacher and her regular teacher. (She attends regular and special educa-tion classes.) They were delighted with the news that Stephanie has covered over a year's grade level in only 6 months' time. Her grade aver-ages in math and reading have improved 1.5 and 1.3 grade levels, respectively.

"Now I can't say that Performance Management did all of this, but I can say that as far as learning in the home, which is a lot of a child's education, it has helped tremendously," Janoulis stated. "She has also recognized that this is helping her, and that's probably the best rein-forcement. Her self-esteem has just shot up," he added.

Because Stephanie's scores sometimes plunged, Janoulis found that a graph discouraged her. Instead, he gives her continual verbal feedback and tracks her test results. "A child with a learning disability gets tested quite frequently to monitor their progress," he remarked.

Janoulis outlined the four main ways that the Performance Management process helped the family work with Stephanie's learning disability:

1. It provided good information on her attention span, her grades, and her behavior that we could give to the psychologists and psychiatrists, pediatricians and teachers on Stephanie's learning disability so that it could be identified.
2. It monitored her progress with her attention span, which was a big problem.
3. It taught us how to pinpoint, how to get the emotionalism out of being a parent. We could look at the problem, identify the problem, and develop the plan.
4. It taught us how to break a big task down into small units, into definitive steps that could be reinforced when we used the flashcards.

Janoulis also had some R+ in the way of positive comments for all of Stephanie's teachers and the school system. "We have had Stephanie in private schools most of her life. Then we moved here to Atlanta. I can't say enough good things about my daughter's school, Dolvin Elementary. They're super." Then he added, "Performance Management, Candy Parrish [her special education teacher], and the Fulton County Board of Education have all been tremendous!"

THE ACE BEHAVIOR MODIFIER MEETS THE PILLSBURY DOUGHBOY: A CASE STUDY[3]

John J. Parrino, Ph.D.

I first saw Ms. P on the maximum security ward of the state hospital. While working with the head nurse on a treatment plan, my attention was admittedly diverted by a 200-pound nude woman standing in the middle of the ward. She was engaged in inappropriate behavior—the kind of behavior that gets people into state hospitals—such as talking to yourself and smacking someone important. At this hospital, Ms. P's behavior landed her an introduction to three psychiatric aides. As they led Ms. P to time-out, I heard her request in a Truman Capote voice, "Poke me in the stomach; I'm the Pillsbury Doughboy."

Famous people were common on this particular ward. We had presidents, kings and queens, FBI directors, and a deity or two. Ms. P, however, was our first Pillsbury Doughboy. One of our problems was that she ran amok (and nude) throughout the ward, soliciting pokes from stunned staff members, other patients, and even the cafeteria ladies.

As the ward consultant, I was affectionately known as the Ace Behavior Modifier. Disruptive patients were invariably assigned to me. My team had a reputation for bringing about speedy behavior change through positive means. Therefore, when other staff plans failed, I volunteered the services of my behavioral team.

The job, in our eyes, was simple. Ms. P would be rewarded with praise and tokens (exchangeable at the hospital's department store) for appropriate behavior. Of course, we only expected her to progress one small step at a time. To earn rewards she had to make only slight improvements such as wearing socks or even a small hat. Later, she had to remain fully dressed to receive the payoff.

With tokens in hand and praise at the tip of our tongues, my team and I stood ready to "catch" Ms. P with her clothes on. And of course, we did. She slept in her clothes, sometimes bathed in them, but in the public view of the ward, her garments were nowhere to be seen.

Frustration set in. Changing behavior in graduate school was easy. A pellet of food to a rat at just the right time caused him to dance across the cage like Chuck Berry. Of course, Ms. P was a human being, but I knew that reinforcement worked with people, too. Why, then, couldn't I change Ms. P's behavior?

Undaunted, my team brainstormed the next obvious step. If we couldn't get Ms. P to dress on the ward, we would dress her ourselves and then reward her. It was one of the oldest behavioral principles: Prompt behavior and reinforce the heck out of it.

"Attention, Code P on Ward L. Repeat, Code P on Ward L."

My first call rang through the corridors of the hospital, a cleverly disguised message meaning, " Help! Bring Ms. P's clothes!" My final report to the staff was a mixed review. The good news was that dressing Ms. P and then rewarding her worked ... temporarily. The bad news was that soon thereafter she sabotaged our plan by forcing us into the mass production of clothing. She flushed them, burned them, and nailed them to the office doors of all the team members, including mine. I knew the end of our intervention was near when Ms. P (masquerading as the Doughboy) barged into a staff meeting screaming, "Yah ha," as she twirled her underwear about her head in cowboy rodeo fashion. Only my quick reflexes saved the chief psychiatrist from a very embarrassing encounter with Ms. P's lingerie.

I was despondent. Had I, the Ace Behavior Modifier, met my match? I paced up and down the ward, which by now had become Ms. P's personal nudist camp. I was ready to throw in the towel, when much to my surprise, Ms. P approached me. "Doctor," she said in Doughboy voice, "why don't you and your team just leave me alone?" And with that, she punched me (with gusto) in the stomach.

As I lay on the floor, Ms. P's words rang in my ears. "Just leave me alone. Just leave me alone." Then it came to me. That was it! If you don't like a behavior, ignore it. Eventually, without reinforcement, it will extinguish.

We tried that plan of action, and it worked. Ms. P. streaked the ward a few more times, but now, with all the staff members going about their usual business, her behavior weakened and then died. Thanks to Ms. P, my reputation remained intact. Was Ms. P a smarter behavioral manager than I was? Maybe so, maybe not, but she taught me a valuable lesson. If you really want to know what will strengthen or weaken a behavior, what will reinforce or punish, just ask. Your patient (your customer, your client, or your employee) will always let you know.

WHAT DO YOU REALLY WANT, TEACHER[4]

Gail Snyder

Ken Sparks is a good student enrolled in his elementary school's Discovery classes, a special program for gifted students. His grades are predominantly N's and B's, though he has made an occasional C in mathematics. He also plays tennis and other sports avidly. All in all he's simply an all-around American boy.

So his mother, Jane Sparks, didn't worry at first when he began to bring home several N's, for "needs to improve," in conduct. Once she contacted the teachers, they assured her that Ken wasn't disruptive or rude but simply had a tendency to gab too much.

And actually, the specific areas that Ken received nonsatisfactory marks in related more to his organization and study skills than his deportment. Ken received N's in conduct categories such as listens well, follows direction, is self-disciplined, completes work on time, uses time wisely, and works well alone. So far, however, these marks hadn't affected Ken's grades negatively.

Yet as the year wore on, his mother noticed that more N's appeared on each successive report card. She talked to Ken, but as yet the teachers had given her no reason to believe that a serious problem existed. Finally, on his third quarter report card, Ken brought home a grand total of 12 N's, a number that had tripled since the first of the school year. But the real clincher was the F in math.

"At first the N's weren't bothering his grades and I knew he wasn't misbehaving, so I wasn't worried," said Jane. "But when he brought home that third quarter report, I went up there. I wanted to see all of the data they had."

Once at the school Jane found that Ken scored in the high 90s, if not 100, on all of his tests. But the teacher showed her a stack of papers removed from Ken's desk that accounted for all of the zeros that had pulled down his grade, even though much of the work was completed. Ken also received zeros for handing in incomplete homework or in some cases not completely following the written directions on a quiz.

For example, in many cases, he got the right answers, but rather than underline the correct answer and write it down, he had only underlined it. Hence, another lower grade for failing to follow instructions. One teacher told Jane that when given free time, Ken read a book rather than work on his homework. Because of this, the teacher gave him an N in "uses time wisely."

But Ken's most significant problem was that he failed to hand in his papers even when he had completed the work. Ken's teacher assured his mother that she did ask for the papers regularly, but that Ken didn't hear her or didn't pay attention. "Their theory is that the consequence is if you give the child instructions and if the child doesn't hear it, then maybe he'll learn something when and if he fails," said Jane. "I know consequences work, but I don't see letting him fail. Maybe the pinpoint for that child is not clear."

Jane is a former teacher herself and her husband has been teaching for over 20 years in the DeKalb County school system, so she can empathize with the heavy workload that teachers carry. However, letting her son fail a subject to learn a lesson in study skills was where she drew the line. At the teacher's urging she set up an appointment with the school psychologist, who told her, "Let the boy fail. Let him see how that feels. His classmates will make fun of him, and that will hurt. Then maybe he will do better."

"Well, I didn't approve of that at all," said Jane.

She went to Aubrey Daniels, a consultant, who after listening to her story agreed to help her set up a matrix for her 10-year-old son. Obviously, Ken was bright enough to do the work, so his main problem was that he didn't hand it in. "We set up a matrix where he would earn points for the behaviors that, obviously, if he did them, his grades were bound to go up," said Jane.

Ken could earn five points for writing down and bringing home all of his homework assignments for the day. He could earn five more points for completing the work. The big 10-pointer required him to hand in the assignment and have his teacher initial the assignment sheet. "He didn't like that part of it, but he was able to manage," said

Jane, "because that was the only way he could earn 10 points out of a possible 20 per day, or 100 per week." Jane also gave Ken extra points for bringing home his graded papers to be signed. "That was another problem. He had not brought many of his papers home to be signed. If his father or I didn't sign a paper, he got a zero even if he had already done the work, handed it in, and the teacher had graded it."

The first week of the matrix Ken and his mother set the goal at 75 points. If he reached the goal, he could play in his Saturday baseball league. If not, he forfeited that privilege. Jane soon discovered that Ken had no problems earning the points. In fact, during the first week, he overachieved by bringing in all of the backlogged papers that had so long been crammed into his desk. (He could earn 1 point for every paper—even a PTA announcement—that he brought home.) But Jane wanted to begin by reinforcing the behavior of simply bringing school-related papers home—any papers.

One of Ken's teachers told her that the three smartest children in her class, those whom she considered to be very gifted (including Ken), had the worst organization. This further assured Jane that she had pin-pointed the correct behaviors for Ken's performance improvement plan.

Jane placed Ken's checklist and graph on his study desk at home. Each week they set higher point goals, and each week Ken achieved them. He seemed to enjoy the responsibility of writing his score on the matrix himself. Besides giving hugs, kisses, encouragement, and approval as Ken progressed Jane also had him make up a reinforcer list for meeting milestones. These included *Mad* magazines, Hardy Boys "Case File" books, and Nerds Blizzards. "That's a horrible thing—candy dumped on top of ice cream and mixed together," explained Jane.

On one 3-day school week Ken had to earn 80 points to go on a Discovery class field trip to the space center in Huntsville, Alabama. He overachieved again despite the shortened school week. Later, Jane received a glowing letter from his teacher about how much better Ken was doing. At year's end Ken received a total of four N's, whittled by two-thirds since the third quarter. He also had three A's, two B's, and one C, up from an F, in math. Ironically, Ken made such high scores on his math aptitude tests that the school is placing him in a seventh grade accelerated course next year, even though he will only be in the sixth grade at that time.

He never came right out and admitted to his mom that her performance improvement plan had made a positive difference, but she could tell that he recognized that fact. "After a short while, it wasn't an ordeal for me to ask for that paper to sign," she said. "He'd bring it out right away and show it to me. I didn't have to dig through his books to find it anymore."

Jane plans to use the system next year, but with some changes. "I don't know if we will use the exact same point system or how we'll work it, but we aren't going to start with nothing, because I think he still needs some guidance." She is very proud of Ken for bringing up his grades and improving his organization and study skills. Finally, his placement exams show her that she has no need to worry about his abilities.

Jane believes her son has learned a very valuable lesson. "I think that the performance improvement plan encouraged him. It showed him that he can."

EDUCATION FOR INMATES REDUCES RECIDIVISM[5]

Gail Snyder

The U.S. prison population has tripled since 1970 with total state and federal spending exceeding $19 billion annually. We appear to be a nation trapped in a repeating cycle of imprisonment, parole, and reimprisonment. Despite the diversity of political views and personal stances on the crime issue, most Americans reach consensus on one point—our present system isn't working.

At least one institution, Wilmington College in Wilmington, Ohio, believes that education plays a key role in preventing repeat offenses from occurring after parole.

Studies show that 41 percent of all prisoners in this country have less than a ninth-grade education, an educational level at which only 16 percent of the adult U.S. population functions. In fact, two-thirds of parolees who return to prison are unemployed, often due to low educational skills. Wilmington College began offering off-campus educational programs at several Ohio correctional institutions in an effort to affect the recidivism rate of parolees. The programs have yielded positive results. In fact, the college programs lower recidivism rates (1 year from parole) from over 30 percent to 11 percent.

Susan Hersh, chair of the education department at Wilmington, explained that the college operates branch campuses in at least three different prisons in Ohio: the Warren Correctional, Lebanon Correctional, and Franklin County System (a state facility for women). "Inmates are able to earn a 4-year degree taking the same courses they would on the main campus," says Hersh. "The courses are taught whenever possible by faculty who also teach on the main campus." Hersh recently taught a class on behavioral learning theory to a group of inmates at the Warren Correctional Institute, a close security (one step below maximum-security) facility in Lebanon, Ohio. There she tried an innovative assignment. She asked the inmates to write a paper based on their new knowledge of behavioral methods with this theme: "If the warden were a behaviorist, how would the prison be run?"

The students (many with records including armed assault, robbery, rape, kidnapping, and murder) came up with some insightful suggestions. "My guess is that most of these guys have been in prison four or five times," said Hersh. "Many of them talked from a practical standpoint that the public would never accept anything other than punishment and that they had to be punished."

In fact, many questions have been raised about "rewarding" criminals with a free education at taxpayers' expense. "The more education they may have, the less likely they are to go back," said Hersh. "The recidivism is definitely lower." Research on postsecondary correctional education reveals that it costs $30,000 per year (and rising) to incarcerate an inmate. Because of the lower recidivism rates, every 100 inmates graduating from college saves the public $570,000.

One interesting aspect of the study was the reinforcers that the prisoners felt would be effective in maintaining a more positive prison environment. "Obviously, early release was the first one," said Hersh. "That was followed by conjugal visits. A few talked about having their own cells. Because of the overcrowded conditions, single cells are no longer available, but they thought there could be very effective changes made if having a single cell were a contingency." Another reinforcer frequently mentioned was extra visiting time and a more efficient structure for arranging visitation appointments.

The prisoners' remarks resulted in "A Behavioral Approach to Prison Reform: A View from the Inmates," a paper presented at the International Conference for Behavior Analysts. In that paper Hersh concluded, "The recidivism rate for graduates of the program is below 12 percent. Most graduates have found employment after their release and many have become advocates for prisoners' rights. Courses in Applied Behavior Analysis (rather than one class) could benefit not only those who take the course, but also the entire prison community for whom they become advocates."

DISHING OUT PM AT THE TARTAN PARK 3M CLUB[6]

Gail Snyder

The Tartan Park 3M Club, a private club for 3M personnel, employs about half a dozen dishwashers 16 to 17 years old. Realizing that washing dishes can be a tedious task, Neil Reinert set out to add sparkle to the chore and cut down on the high turnover rate for dishwashers at the club.

Putting his PM training to work, Reinert first monitored the employees for several weeks in order to set up pinpoints for good performance and establish a baseline for the Performance Management program. He soon had a list of pinpoints for monitoring the dishwashers. The program is based on a point system with verbal and tangible reinforcement.

Some of the pinpoints are mopping the floor at night, running the bus pans through the washer, and checking the silverware. (The silverware cleanliness is also monitored by the waitresses.) After devising the checklist and point system he hung a graph in the dishwashing room. Because the dishwashers usually worked in teams of two or more, Reinert decided that the teamwork route was the best to follow. "At the very beginning of the program there was a notable change," he said. "The employees were really enthused. The slower ones soon realized that they had to pick up the pace to achieve the goal."

If the goal was achieved for 3 weeks in a row, each person would receive the reinforcement of a $15 gift certificate redeemable for 3M gift products and clothing, theater tickets, Northstar hockey tickets, or dinner at the club. Working as a team and encouraging one another, the entire dishwashing staff achieved the goal quickly. So far the most popular reinforcer is hockey tickets.

Brenda Bouchie, a 16-year-old student and worker at the 3M Club, feels that the program is working well. "It puts more incentive into us to do our job better. It has helped a lot because people work harder and everything's cleaner. The cooks come in and grade us in the morning, and they've had a lot of compliments from the other employees about how much better everything looks," she said.

Since the start-up of the program, Brenda has noticed a difference in herself and her fellow workers: "People are more excited. They started doing things they don't normally do. Instead of just sitting there and waiting for something to do, they find things to do—clean up. I noticed it in myself, too."

Brenda used her first gift certificate for hockey tickets. She explained that the top prize right now is a 3M jacket: "We're all working hard to get that." Brenda said that she would use PM if she ever managed people: "It brings more enthusiasm to the workers and helps them work together more as a team. The atmosphere is a lot nicer."

Brenda Kluge, 17, another worker at the 3M Club, adds, "It gave us something to look forward to. When we heard about what we could do with the gift certificates, we really wanted to get them. So we worked real hard to get our points. Everybody started to work together better, too. If someone was moving a little slow, we'd say, 'Remember, we can get that.' We'd work harder and look at the point sheet every day. The checklist helps because we use it to make sure we have certain things done. Now we know exactly what to do."

Reinert said, "Since we started [PM], we haven't had a turnover yet. They're happy to come to work and look forward to achieving the goal as a team."

STRUCTURED WITH LOVE:
PM AND VICTIMIZED CHILDREN[7]

Gail Snyder

When David Swanger and his wife, Skippy, decided to work at the Presbyterian Children and Family Ministries of Alabama, they intended to stay for only 1 year. At that time, Skippy told her husband, "After 1 year if we can tell ourselves that we've helped one child, let's be satisfied."

That was over 3 years ago, and the Swangers are still hard at work as cottage counselors to eight boys ages 10 to 14. "We feel that we've been able to help a lot more than one child," said David. "But let me say right away that without Performance Management, we wouldn't be there."

Several years ago, David retired from Kimberly-Clark Corporation after 35 years as a process-control engineer. During a visit to their grandchildren, the Swangers' son-in-law, Russell Justice, performance manager at Tennessee Eastman, invited David to a 1-day PM seminar. "I went and I thoroughly enjoyed it," David said. "Two things caught my eye: one, Russell's enthusiasm for PM, and two, the parallels between PM and what I had been doing for 35 years in process-control engineering."

The Swangers may never have thought of PM again if they hadn't later run head on into a "chaotic situation." Skippy Swanger has been an active volunteer for many years. After retiring, David joined her. The two had raised three children of their own and over the years also had opened their home to three sets of foster children. So when a friend suggested the couple might enjoy working at a local ranch for troubled boys, they agreed to try. "That's when we came face to face with chaos," admitted David.

The Swangers found that the boys, many accustomed to little discipline and from troubled backgrounds, were almost uncontrollable. Several days later, they asked their son-in-law, "Do you think we could develop a PM system for child care?" They spent that weekend designing their first PM system. "What we are now doing has evolved from that beginning," explained David.

Today the Swangers, even though they own a home of their own, live as surrogate parents to Gabbie Cottage located on the main campus of the Presbyterian Home for Children in Talladega, Alabama.

The nonprofit home serves some 100 children per year, children whose families are broken due to unemployment, mental illness, and imprisonment, as well as physical, emotional, drug, and sexual abuse. The Presbyterian Home, which has been in operation for 125 years, provides ranch-style living quarters, a large dining hall, a gymnasium, a swimming pool, and an educational center for the victimized children.

"It is the mission of the ministry to reconcile children with their families if they can," explained David. "However, in most cases that's just not practical. In fact, they must be separated.

"When we first got into child care we discovered that victimized children are very difficult to manage. Though you may have a great desire to nurture those children and get them into some system where you can help them, you can't do that just by having the desire. You've got to get scientific with it, and PM is the tool that we use. Believe me, children are capable of the most awful misbehavior."

At Gabbie Cottage, the Swangers put together a simple point system for the resident family members. Each child can earn 7 points a day, 1 point for each of seven categories, for a maximum of 49 points per week. The number of points the child earns determines what his or her privileges are for the day, and at week's end, the cumulative score determines weekend privileges.

Each night the Swangers sit down and score the children. If a child earns a point for a category, he receives a highlighted X.

"There are usually only one or two infractions a day, if any, so I ran off the score sheets with the Xs already on them, which doesn't mean that the children earn the points inherently. I did that so that keeping score wouldn't become discouraging to the house parents. So that they wouldn't have to make 99 million X's a night," explained David.

The children know exactly what they have to do to earn the points. If they don't remember, they are quickly reminded, because the Swangers mark out the X and write out the specific reason the point wasn't earned. "It's real easy for them to earn the point," said David. "If they are doing it approximately right, then they earn the point for that day. We're not trying to make them look bad. We're trying to make them look good. We reward successive approximations. And by doing that we have proved to ourselves that the process works. If you've wondered if shaping really works, we can tell you now that it does."

There is no guessing about earned privileges, either. The Schedule of Rewards hangs directly above the daily score sheets. Consequently, each child knows early each morning what list of activities he can choose from that day. "That score sheet is like a watering hole," said David. "I wouldn't move it a quarter of an inch from where it belongs, because they [the children] are going to be there."

David created two cartoon characters: Knucklehead Brown (K.B.) for the boys and Georgia Brown for the girls. He uses these characters to get messages across to the children, tell jokes, and give them something to discuss. He also writes riddles and sticks stars on the score sheets.

"The kids get involved in this, and they get to be a part of it," he said. One night he sketched a cartoon of his dog Bob saying, "Once upon a time in a dream of mine, a billygoat made a 49." This prompted the comment from one little boy, "Well, if a billygoat can make 49, so can I."

Aunt Skippy and Uncle David, as some of the children call them, also enhance the points by highlighting the scores in red—the higher the score, the more intense the color. "And if you forget to highlight a score, they'll tell you in a hurry," said David.

The scoring ends every Thursday at midnight, so on Friday morning each child knows his weekend privileges. The Swangers also created another fun reward—the grab bag—for any child who scores a perfect score of 49 by week's end. Uncle David usually makes up the grab bags, stuffing them with anything from authentic arrowheads to old English coins. He always makes up one extra bag so that even the last child has a choice.

David tapes a dollar bill on the bottom of one of the grab bags. Whoever gets that dollar bill not only gets to keep the money but wins the extra grab bag as well. "They try to fathom our thinking and try to decide which one of those bags has the dollar bill on it," he said. "That adds to the excitement."

Although competition among the children is discouraged, Uncle David had to make one small concession. When he started the score sheets, he placed the names on the sheet in random order. One boy, whose scores had been low, asked, "Why is my name on the bottom of the sheet?"

David decided that the boy had made a valid observation. He promised to put the boy's name on the top of the sheet the following week if he earned the highest score that week. David's been arranging the names according to the previous week's scores ever since. Those with the highest scores have their full names listed at the top of the sheet. To offset that bit of competition, however, he uses a system that allows everyone to profit when even one person makes a perfect score.

Every time a child earns a perfect weekly score the Swangers put 2 cents in a money jar. The amount of money in the jar is growing rapidly, and the children are excited about it. Why? Because one of these days somebody is going to make a perfect score, get a grab bag, and be lucky enough to get the bag with the dollar bill. That child will then win the money in the jar, but only IF everyone else that week has made a perfect score.

The Swangers also use a points and reinforcement plan to encourage the children to concentrate on their studies. Noting that usually the children who scored A's and B's at school received the most coverage in the campus newsletter, David suggested that those children who had improved also be recognized. Almost immediately the campus added that section to its newsletter, featuring the photos and names of the students who showed academic improvement over the last grading period.

In Gabbie Cottage the Swangers began graphing the cumulative grade point averages of the children, setting challenging but attainable improvement goals and giving the children a list of rewards to choose from when they achieved those goals. Although some skeptics scoffed at the idea of graphing cumulative scores, the scores at Gabbie Cottage soon rose steadily.

The campus has a total of six residential cottages, a shelter system, and a therapeutic treatment center. "We are very pleased that in five of those eight residential buildings we've installed PM," said David.

The shelter system may house children for as little as several hours or for as long as 2 weeks, but generally the turnover is quite rapid. The therapeutic center helps those children who have been so victimized, they don't yet feel secure in a public school setting. Those children go to school on campus until they are ready to move into the residential cottages.

Both the shelter system and the therapeutic center modified the Swangers' point system to suit their needs. For example, the therapeutic center includes points for academics and in-class behavior as well as at-home behavior. The Swangers never try to force the Performance Management process on new house parents or counselors. David explained: "We found out that imposing PM doesn't work. We wait around for somebody to ask us, 'What can you do for us?' Then we say, 'Let's you and I sit down and see what we can work out.' That way they become part of the process, part of developing the system. They are much more likely to use the system if you do it that way. And in every case that they've tried it, it has worked. It works just as well in one cottage as it does in another."

All house parents receive a guide to the parenting methods the home advocates. The guide includes an explanation of Performance Management, detailing how and why it works. The Swangers give much credit to the Presbyterian Children and Family Ministries for backing the PM process.

"Most of them have examined child care point systems used at other institutions, but those systems are often so complicated that neither the counselors nor the children really understood them."

"There isn't a lot of hassle or questions about this system," said David. "They understand it perfectly. The children see that there is a spectrum of responses to their performance ... the better their performances, the more things will come their way."

These cottage parents use the same nonconfrontational philosophy with their cottage children, especially newcomers. They don't philosophize or tell a newcomer that he must earn points and so on. They simply let him observe and find out for himself what all the excitement is about. "They catch on pretty quickly that what they want to do is contingent upon them doing what we want them to do," said David. He emphasizes that while he may be the engineer, he considers his wife to be the operator.

"The word *contingency* is at the heart of just about everything she does," he's quick to point out. "No Performance Management system operates itself. It has to be implemented by a person, a surrogate parent in this case. The person most capable of doing that is the person who uses the authoritative style, the parent who says I'll give the child freedom within certain limits. I'll exercise control over the child, but I'll be warm and receptive at the same time, and I'll encourage independence. All I want him to do is follow some rules, live in some kind of structure. This gives me the opportunity to shape him. You want him to be independent, self-reliant, well adjusted, and you can have that kind of a child, even if he's been victimized in the past."

David and Skippy do not see themselves as saints for giving their time to create a secure home life for these children. They genuinely enjoy it, though Skippy admits, "Anybody in child care asks themselves at least once every 6 months, 'How in the world did I ever get in this line of work?'"

But David added, "What we're doing in Performance Management would not be working without the benefit of her input and her abilities with children. She is a master at PM, and she also has an innate ability to manage children, to understand contingency, and ... she loves them, too."

ENDNOTES

CHAPTER 1

1. K. Ericsson, R. Krampe, and C. Tesch-Romer, "The Role of Deliberate Practice in the Acquisition of Expert Performance." *Psychological Review* 3: 364, 1993.
2. B. F. Skinner, "Intellectual Self-Management in Old Age." *American Psychologist* 3: 239–244, 1983.
3. B. F. Skinner, *Beyond Freedom and Dignity.* New York: Vintage, 1971.

CHAPTER 3

1. Mark Twain, The Adventures of *Huckleberry Finn.* New York: Harper & Brothers, 1899.

CHAPTER 4

1. Henry Wheeler Shaw (pen name of Josh Billings), *Proverbs, Farmer's Allminax,* 1874.
2. Richard P. Feynman, *"What Do You Care What Other People Think?": Further Adventures of a Curious Character.* Bantam Doubleday Dell, 1992.

CHAPTER 5

1. The literature and research on the ABC model is extensive. For readers who want more detailed and technical explanation, refer to A. C. Daniels, *Performance Management: Improving Quality Productivity through Positive Reinforcement*, 3d ed. Tucker, GA: Performance Management Publications, 1989, or W. David Pierce and W. Frank Epling, *Behavior Analysis and Learning*, 2d ed. Upper Saddle River, NJ: Prentice-Hall, 1999.

CHAPTER 6

1. Sophocles, *Tereus*, c.495 BC

CHAPTER 7

1. Mark Twain, *A Tramp Abroad*. New York: P. F. Collier & Co., 1921.
2. Dio Chrysostom, *Eleventh Discourse*.
3. Robert Epstein, "Extinction-Induced Resurgence: Preliminary Investigations and Possible Applications." *Psychological Record*, 2: 143–153, 1986.

CHAPTER 9

1. Bobby Jones, *Golf Is My Game*. New York: Doubleday, p. 90, 1960.
2. Reprinted with the permission of Simon & Schuster from *The Autobiography of Benjamin Franklin*, p. 139. Copyright © 1962 by Macmillan Publishing Co., Inc., copyright © renewed 1997 by Simon & Schuster.
3. David Premack, "Toward Empirical Behavior Laws: I. Positive Reinforcement…" *Psychological Review*, 4: 219–233, 1959.

CHAPTER 10

1. Alfie Kohn, *Punished by Rewards.* Boston: Houghton, Mifflin, 1993.
2. M. H. Popkin, "Active Parenting: A Video Based Program." In M. J. Fine et al. (eds.), *The Second Handbook on Parent Education: Contemporary Perspectives.* San Diego, CA: Academic Press, 1989.

CHAPTER 11

1. Mark Twain, *Pudd'nhead Wilson's Calendar.* London: Chatto & Windus, 1894.
2. K. R. Johnson and T. V. J. Layng, "Breaking the Structuralist Barrier: Literacy and Numeracy with Fluency." *American Psychologist,* 11: 1473–1490, 1992.
3. B. F. Skinner, *The Technology of Teaching.* New York: Appleton-Century-Crofts, 1968.
4. R. Eisenberger, "Learned Industriousness." *Psychological Review.* 99: 248–267, 1992.
5. J. B. Watson, *Behaviorism.* New York. Norton, 1930 and 1970.
6. D. C. McClelland, *The Achieving Society.* New York: Free Press, 1961.
7. B. Hart and T. R. Risley, *Meaningful Differences in the Everyday Experiences of Young American Children.* Baltimore: Paul H. Brookes, 1995.
8. T. R. Risley, Unpublished study, 1968.

CHAPTER 12

1. Ogden Lindsley, "From Technical Jargon to Plain English for Application." *Journal of Applied Behavior Analysis,* 3: 449–458, 1991.

2. Otto Fenichel, *The Psychoanalytical Theory of Neurosis*. New York: Norton, 1945.
3. Reprinted with the permission of Simon & Schuster from *The Autobiography of Benjamin Franklin*, pp. 82–84. Copyright © 1962 by Macmillan Publishing Co., Inc., copyright © renewed 1997 by Simon & Schuster.

CHAPTER 13

1. L. E. Acker, B. C. Goldwater, and J. L. Agnew, "Sidney Slug: A Computer Simulation for Teaching Shaping without an Animal Laboratory." *Teaching of Psychology*, 2: 130–132, 1990.
2. Reprinted with the permission of Simon & Schuster from *The Autobiography of Benjamin Franklin*. Copyright © 1962 by Macmillan Publishing Co., Inc., copyright © renewed 1997 by Simon & Schuster.

CHAPTER 14

1. David Thompson, *Managing People, Influencing Behavior*, St. Louis: Mosby, p. 9, 1978.
2. Murray Sidman, *Coercion and Its Fallout*. Boston: Authors Cooperative, 1989.
3. Dale Carnegie, *How to Win Friends and Influence People* (1936). New York: Simon & Schuster, 1982.
4. Thompson.

CHAPTER 15

1. Janis Allen, *I Saw What You Did and I Know Who You Are*. Atlanta: Performance Management Publications, pp. 164–165, 1990.

2. P. Levin and A. Isen, "Further Studies on the Effect of Feeling Good on Helping." *Sociometry,* 38, 1975.

CHAPTER 16

1. C. H. Madsen, Jr. and C. R. Madsen, *Teaching and Discipline: Behavior Principles toward a Positive Approach.* Boston: Allyn & Bacon, 1974.
2. R. B. Stuart, "Assessment and Change of the Communication Patterns of Juvenile Delinquents and Their Parents," *Advances in Behavior Therapy.* New York: Academic Press, 1971.
3. R. M. Axelrod, *The Evolution of Cooperation.* New York: Basic Books, 1984.
4. H. G. Wells, *Phoenix.* London: Secker & Warburg, 1942.

APPENDIX

1. *Performance Management,* 9(4): 1991, pp. 7–9.
2. *Performance Management,* 6(2): 1988, pp. 19–20.
3. *Performance Management,* 10(4): 1992, pp. 34–35.
4. *Performance Management,* 7(4): 1989, pp. 31–32.
5. *Performance Management,* 11(2): 1993, pp. 31–34.
6. *Performance Management,* 5(2): 1987, pp. 6–7.
7. *Performance Management,* 8(1): 1990, pp. 29–32.

INDEX

ABOUT THE AUTHOR

Aubrey C. Daniels, Ph.D., founder and CEO of Aubrey Daniels International, is a pioneer in introducing the principles of behavioral psychology to the workplace. Internationally recognized as an author, speaker, and expert in behavior-based technologies, Dr. Daniels advises Fortune 500 companies on management and human performance issues such as safety, quality, productivity, compensation and rewards, morale, performance systems, employee education, and change management.

Dr. Daniels' award-winning book *Bringing Out the Best in People: How to Apply the Astonishing Power of Positive Reinforcement* is published by McGraw-Hill and now in its second edition. The book has been translated into three languages. He is also the author of *Performance Management: Improving Quality Productivity through Positive Reinforcement*, which is a standard text in many university business schools. Dr. Daniels has authored and coauthored numerous articles for business magazines and professional journals, is a consulting editor for the *Journal of Organizational Behavior Management*, writes a monthly column on motivation for *Entrepreneur.com magazine*, and is the founder and publisher of *Performance Management Magazine*, now in an online format at www.pmezine.com. He has been featured in numerous local and national publications and has been interviewed by *The Wall Street Journal*, *Fortune*, *Entrepreneur*, Biznet, CNBC, and CBS radio.

Dr. Daniels is an Associate of Harvard University's John F. Kennedy School of Government and is a visiting professor at Florida State, North Texas State, and West Michigan universities. He has also taught at Georgia State University, Emory University, and Atlanta universities. His numerous awards include the Lifetime Achievement Award from the Organizational Behavior Management Network for outstanding work in the behavior analysis field. In 1997, he received an Outstanding Service Award from the International Association for Behavior Analysis. In 1999 he was featured in *The Guru Guide: The Best Ideas of the Top Management Thinkers*.